Đồng Văn
Sapa
Hà Giang
Điện Biên Phủ
Hà Nội
Hạ Long
Hải Phòng
Vinh
Vientiane
(Laos)
Huế
Đà Nẵng
Quảng ngãi
Quy Nhơn
Pleiku
Đà Lạt
Phnohm Penh
(Cambodia)
Hồ Chí Minh city
Long Xuyên
Cần Thơ
Cà Mau

At a glance....

Population: **100 million**

Language: **Vietnamese**

Ethnic groups: **54**
(Kinh are 80% of popn)

Capital: **Hanoi**
(Population 5 million)

Weather: **Tropical**

Traffic: **Right-hand side**, hectic

Electricity: **220 V,
2 pins** (flat or round)

Religion: **Tam Giao**
(Three Together),
Buddhism, Christianity

Government:
Communist (Marxist)

Neighbours: **China, Laos
and Cambodia**

Independence: **1945**

Northern tip: Dong Van

Liberation: **1975**

Southern tip: Ca Mau

Local governments:
58 provinces, 5 cities

Dong Van to Ca Mau:
2,450 km

Most popular attraction:
Halong Bay

National dish: clear
noodle soup **(phở)**

UNESCO World heritage
sites: Eight

Exchange rate (2022):
US$1 buys 23,000 dong

Sim cards: US$10 for one
month (10 GB)

Bunk in dormitory:
$8 per night

Country code: +84

Two star hotel: US$20

3G / 4G coverage (% of
population): 99% / 95%

Four star hotel: US$50

Water: bottled

Names:
Family Middle First

Cheap / premium
restaurant meal:
US$2 / $15

Cheap / premium beer:
US$0.50 / $3

Foreword

Travel recommendations get repeated over and over for just a dozen places in Vietnam. These are amazing places, but… Do you wonder what lies beyond them? Do they represent a little or a lot of Vietnam's diversity? What are those popular locations really like? Are the brochures honest? Were they written in New York, Sydney or Hong Kong?

Vietnam is my second home, and my book relates what I know. It's based on extensive travel and learning from local people about their lives, their land, beliefs and history. So far, I've been to 60 of the 63 provinces, cycled and walked more than 8,000 km, ridden a motorbike (6,000 km) and taken local buses (more than 6,000 km), crisscrossing the nation, happy as a dog with two tails.

My journey began after a friend's visit, and her strong recommendation: "Brett…You'd love Vietnam". Oh? Really? It seemed unlikely. A couple of years later, I flew into Hồ Chí Minh city, booked into a budget hotel and despite being very worried about the traffic, took a trip on a motorbike. As predicted, I loved it. I still do.

The kindness I received from complete strangers was wonderful. Most of that trip I was either on the motorbike or sitting quietly (with no Vietnamese) amongst ordinary people. I saw them banding together to share and help each other. Everyone knew everyone, even in big towns. Children and the elderly were loved and protected. The mountains, beaches and farms rolled by, and I made it into Hà Nội after a marvelous shambles of a journey. The following year, I took three longer, more adventurous trips by bicycle. Then went with friends as an amateur guide on a cycling tour up north in 2016, followed by another in the south in 2017. My friends were engrossed and delighted. I learned that there's something here for everyone.

Now it's my pleasure to give you my travel advice and insights to the land where Heaven touches Earth.

The Lotus flower is Vietnam's national emblem. Although it spends the night deep in mud, it reaches towards the morning light and opens beautiful and unblemished. The petals represent the diverse ethnic groups, and the many provinces and communities that contribute to the nation.

Vietnamese and Buddhist people attach special significance to the lotus as a symbol of karma: the understanding that all actions have consequences, and so a generous person will be given money, a person giving no respect will receive none, and a thief will undoubtedly be robbed.

Photo:
Wikimedia Commons, the free media repository

More about my first trip....

Before I had thought it through, I bought a motorbike in Hồ Chí Minh City with a sketchy plan to take the backroads to Hà Nội (2,000 km). A mechanic added a rack to my motorbike for my backpack - and off I went. Easy!

I'm a big guy, riding a black cruiser bike with high handlebars and a noisy exhaust, and on the edge of the city a schoolkid leans out of a bus and shouts "Hey! Arnie!" Thanks kid! Vroom! Within a few hours the traffic had exhausted me, then a typhoon hit and soaked me to the bone. Now I'm half-lost and starving. My heroic inner 'Arnie' was gone. All I had left was the real me. A guy with a desk job who mostly can't get the printer to work. What have I done? I feel <u>so</u> stupid and inadequate.

Ahead, through the heaviest of pouring rain, there's a roadside eatery. Getting off the bike I stumble on the muddy ground. My gloves wash away down the gutter. I put my head under the blue tarp roof and ask: English? Shaking heads, of course. The cook invites me to sit and does a fine impression of a chicken. So I nod, and in no time there's chicken fried rice. Food has a special flavour when you are starving. And there is a friendly smile too, draining away some of my doubts and upsets. Soon there are glasses and rice whisky and lessons in how to drink it. All at once! The diners, the cook, her sister and her husband are all so disarmingly friendly.

My habits are a source of great fun because I use chopsticks like a pro but don't understand any of the questions I'm asked, and I take the chillies out of my food. The cook looks at the unwanted chillies and waves her hand in front of her mouth as if to say "Too hot for a white guy!". I wave my hand behind my backside and make a painful face: "Too hot back there too!" She bursts into laughter then goes around the tables repeating the joke for everyone and pointing back to me. She's a natural performer and obviously loved by her customers. It's all very funny and we're laughing along together. My spirit has been transported from a grey, numb place into the light and warmth.

More rice, more rice whiskies, more jokes in sign language. I feel like a King.

What is this magic? Who are these people?
Day one is complete; ten to go....

Contents

Introduction

Việt Nam is a mid-sized country of nearly 100 million people, located east of Laos and Cambodia. Việt Nam means "south land", while China and Mongolia are the "north lands". Vietnamese is spoken by about 90 million people - the 12th most common language in the world.

The land area is roughly that of Malaysia, Germany or a combination of Nevada, Colorado and Utah. Not too big, not too small. The landscapes are diverse: steaming swampy jungles in the Mekong Delta to 10,000 feet high mountains in the north that sometimes get snow. There are World Heritage-listed Ha Long Bay and colourful coral reefs in the warm seas. With more than 50 ethnic groups and several religions, this is a multi-cultural country. Minority groups are respected and celebrated for their individual identities as well as their contribution to the national identity. Without a doubt, the greatest natural resources are the people and their spirit of cooperation and hard work.

This book has the tips that I needed on my early trips to Việt Nam. Mostly, it's simple stuff like where and when to go, what's there, what to wear and what to eat. I've included plenty of information about the multitude of cultures and history. Cultural knowledge has added depth to my enjoyment of my most recent visits, so I encourage all visitors to learn as well as look.

Note: Vietnamese and English spelling are similar (Hà Nội is Hà Nội, Vietnam is Việt Nam). I've mainly used Vietnamese spelling.

Travel essentials

At international airports, it's a good idea after passing immigration and customs, to get some Vietnamese Dong (VND) from an ATM. Two million dong are US$80-$100 and sufficient for your immediate needs. Don't carry more than ten million dong in the airport or at border gates.

Your taxi, bus or rideshare driver probably won't speak more than a few words of English, so it helps to have the name and the street address of your accommodation printed on a piece of paper. You may be asked to pay two or three small tolls on the freeway (15,000 dong - less than $1). At the end of a good trip, a tip to the driver and a "thank you" are always welcome. If your driver is speeding, firmly say "charm!" (chậm! "slow!").

Hotel transfers are convenient, and generally cost just $1-$5 more than a taxi. A driver meets you at the front of the terminal and delivers you hassle-free to your accommodation.

- Hà Nội (HAN). Nội Bài airport is 45 km from the city centre (Hoàn Kiếm) and a taxi is ~ 400,000 ($20) regardless of the number of passengers. An orange coloured Transerco bus departs once or twice per hour and costs about $3. It will be marked Bờ Hồ or 'Hoàn Kiếm'. Rideshares (Grab) are available.

- Hồ Chí Minh city (SGN). Tân Sơn Nhất airport is only 7 km from the centre (District 1) and costs ~ 200,000 ($10) in a taxi. The Line 49 bus costs 75,000 ($3) and departs every 30 mins to 1 hour. The taxi booking system is sketchy, so check before or get a hotel transfer.

- Đà Nẵng (DAD). The airport is only 3 km from the city and 5 km from popular Mỹ Khê beach. A taxi to the beachfront costs ~120,000 ($6).
- Phú Quốc Island (PQC). The airport is in the middle of the island. Many hotels and beaches are just 5 km and ~120,000 VND ($6) taxifare from the airport. The furthest are 15-20 km and ~250,000 VND ($12).

Money

The arrival halls of major airports have multi-lingual ATMs dispensing VND. USD$1 varies from 20,000 to 25,000 VND, so 1 M VND is about US$45. The ATMs have low fees (less than $1) but the exchange rates vary quite a lot.

US dollars are a useful backup to your VND, but they aren't useful as a daily currency. For 'insurance' against losing your wallet or luggage, keep $20 or $50 in your bag, coat or shoe. A credit card serves the same purpose. If you remove the CVV number from the back of the credit card, it has a lot less value to a thief. Be sure to memorise it before scratching it off.

Pounds, AUD, CAN etc aren't useful currencies, but make nice gifts for friends and helpful hotel staff. Bank accounts are for residents and frequent visitors only.

Visas and Immigration

Vietnam has e-visas for easy immigration if you're travelling on EU, ASEAN, USA, Australian, NZ and other passports. E-visas have been the first available after the covid-19 pandemic, and are available to passport-holders from 80 countries.

Embassies and consulates may offer the usual visa-from-embassy, though they were stopped during the Covid-19 pandemic. Phone before applying.

The visa-on-arrival is popular when available. Most people have no problem other than a wait at the processing office in the airport. However, watch out for on-line scams with buying a 'Pre-approval letter'.

Advantages of visa-from-embassy and e-visa are no pre-approval letter or fee, less chance of scam, saves time in immigration. Advantages of visa-on-arrival are sometimes a cheaper visa, and sometimes less paperwork.

Geography

Việt Nam is much wider in the north and south than in the middle, so many people say it's the country shaped like an 8 or an S. Indeed, it's only 50 km wide in the central section of the country between Đà Nẵng and Vinh. Central Vietnam has scenic mountains and plateaux to the west of a narrow coastal strip with excellent beaches.

In the south, the Mekong River delivers rich sediment to the Delta during floods each wet season. This sediment builds wonderful soil that grows half of Việt Nam's rice crop: about 20 million tonnes. It's called the "rice bowl" of Việt Nam and sometimes "a gift from God to the people". Three crops are grown each year. In the north, the Red River Valley is the centre of rice production, growing two crops per year either side of the cool weather in winter. The far north has mountain ranges that define the border with China.

Food

Is street and market food safe?

Yes. Food stalls have a good reputation for healthy, tasty food. Restaurants around the world have the occasional problem, and it's possible for things to go wrong here, too. But an old, blackened pot or the dirty footpath is not a guide to the cleanliness of the food itself. If lots of Vietnamese people are eating there, you can rest assured that it has a good reputation for taste and safety. The most common causes of feeling unwell are not food, but dehydration or lack of electrolytes. Some gastric upsets are caused by too much beer, hot chillies or fresh, green vegetables.

How can it be so safe and healthy?

It's not immediately obvious, but local people insist on fresh, clean produce. Vegetables go from the field to the bowl in hours. Bread is baked daily. Any foods kept in storage, such as rice and groceries, are kept bagged.

In the "wet" market all perishable goods are produced and sold locally. Even in the cities, fresh-picked food is taken to the market before dawn. Chickens, ducks, fish and snails are sold live or fresh-cooked. Fresh meat is butchered, sold and cooked on the same day. Stallholders are under great pressure from 'the granny network'* who reject any food that isn't as fresh as when it was picked, caught or laid.

*The "granny network" buys and prepares a huge amount of food daily, especially for working families. They meet or phone often, discussing all things related to shopping, cooking, family, children and grandchildren. Produce that

5

disappoints the grannies will be difficult to sell and the shop will lose money and its reputation.

Side note: In the markets you'll see exotic meats including boar, horse, goat, dog, squirrel, lizard, snake and frog. Many people won't be interested in them. But if you wish to try them, ask a local guide for directions to a restaurant that prepares them well. The guide may also know whether they are farmed or wild animals and whether they received adequate housing and care during their life.

Wild animals in Vietnam are under severe pressure from hunting. Please reject any offer of "forest" or "wild" meat.

Pho' (pronounced 'fur') is the national dish, and bún is a close second (the 'u' is pronounced like the 'u' in 'put'). The rice noodles in phở are flat (as in the photo) and bún are round. The differences in flavour are mainly due to the

way the broth is made (usually phở is from beef and bún from pork).

Phở is prepared by simmering lean beef and bones (ribs or legs) for at least 4 hours. The distinctive aroma and flavours begin with a satchel of fresh-roasted spices that goes in the pot with the bones. There'll be cinnamon, star anise, ginger or galangal, red shallots and mustard seeds. The broth is regularly skimmed to maximise clarity. Cooking starts during the night, so it's ready for early morning customers. It is a centuries-old process involving secret recipes and a long-running rivalry between Hà Nội and Hồ Chí Minh city.

Assorted styles are served with beef (bo), chicken (ga) or tofu (dofu). Just before serving, the phở noodles are heated and very lightly cooked for a few seconds and poured into the bowl over the meat and veggies (onion, yam). It's served with salad greens including mungbeans (green beans) sprouts, mint, perilla (alligator mint), Vietnamese mint (cilantro), lemon grass. Flavourings include fresh lime, garlic, chilli and sauces (fish, soy, chilli). There are dozens of popular styles, but the most popular among tourists are:

- phở Hà Nội (also known as phở bắc)
- phở bò Huế (and bún bò Huế)
- phở Nam (also known as phở Sài Gòn).

Bún is less well-known overseas than phở, but it is just as good, or better. The most popular is bún chả, made from rich, slightly salty pork broth and containing pieces of pork belly and little balls of pork mince. Like phở it will come with and abundance of herbs and sauces.

To find the best phở and bún places near where you are staying, consult the front desk of your accommodation or a local guide. In the Hà Nội old quarter there are dozens and dozens of choices. There is a good one at the corner of Hàng Trống and Hang Gai, called Phở Bưng Hàng Trống and another not far away at 10 Lý Quốc Sư called, predictably, Phở 10 Lý Quốc Sư. There's an old family bún restaurant about 2 km west of the lake at Ngõ 14, 59 Láng Hạ, Đống Đa. Here at Bún Chả Hương Liên 2, you can order the "Obama Combo" that US president Obama chose when dining here with chef and food guide Anthony Bourdain. Bourdain has said that his favourite cuisine is Vietnamese and that this is one of his favourite restaurants. High praise! If you can't get there, or it's packed out, there's also a Bún Chả Hương Liên at 24 Lê Văn Hưu. In Hồ Chí Minh city, Phở Hoa Pasteur is popular and easy to find at 260C Pasteur Street. The restaurant doesn't look special, but the food is consistently divine, in my opinion.

The central region has some styles, too, including one of the very best: Mì Quảng. Based on smoky barbeque chicken, you should be able to get it in Đà Nẵng, Huế and Quảng Ngãi. Is it the best of all? Maybe!

Bánh mì (pronounced 'barng mee') is a Vietnamese sandwich. They're served all day in the cities and for breakfast from roadside stalls, bus stations, tourist attractions and anywhere that a crowd can be found. The name means 'bread' and 'sandwich' which fails to convey how good they are. For an outlay of $1 to $3 it's cheap, fairly healthy, outstanding value and a pleasantly familiar option.

The small baguette is crispy on the outside and soft inside, due to a unique combination of high-strength flour, raising agents and extended kneading and stretching to give it extra "body". There are many fillings, including sliced or shredded pork, chicken, egg, omelette, beef, duck, tofu,

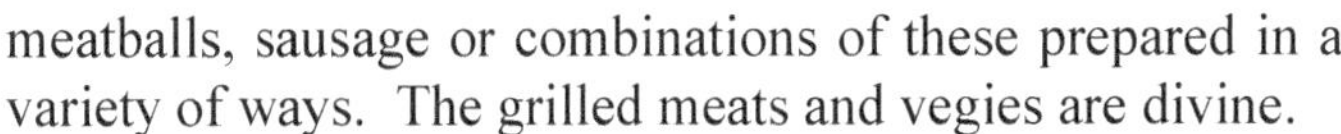

meatballs, sausage or combinations of these prepared in a variety of ways. The grilled meats and vegies are divine.

Fine-cut cucumber, carrot, sprouts, pickled vegetables and coriander create crunch and a mix of Asian and European flavours. The sauces include pate, 'mayonnaise', light soy, fish and chilli. There are also some types of bánh mì that depart from this general description. In the south there's one with pork broth poured over the filling. The first time I saw this I thought 'That's wrong' (it'll ruin the baguette) but it was *delicious*. Regrettably, I don't know of a bánh mì kitchen in the cities that make this one. As far as I've experienced them, they are more common in small-town markets and bus stops in southern Vietnam.

The best and friendliest service of bánh mì in Hà Nội is at Bánh Mì 25 at 25 Hàng Cá street. There are many options here, including vegetarian and a new style: bánh mì in a bowl with baguettes on the side. They're proving a hit. Breakfast here is a bucket-list experience. Add a drip coffee with fresh or condensed milk to set you up for a day exploring the Old Quarter of the city.

The best banh mi in Hồ Chí Minh city is at the much-loved Banh Mi Huỳnh Hoa at 26 Lê Thị Riêng Street. They open mid-afternoon and sell until they run out a few hours later. There are long queues and lots of celebrity gossip at this place. Take care with their hot chilli sauce. People in Hồ Chí Minh city enjoy hot and spicy. Update: The shop has split into two. They are both great. A range of bánh mì franchises have established themselves in most cities in recent years, serving traditional and new styles.

Spring rolls are another favourite. They're small, either fresh or fried. Although pork or pork and prawn are popular, vegetarian options are very good, too. All are delicious and affordable.

The photo shows fried vegetarian spring rolls ("Nem zzang chay" or "Nem rrang chay" in the south). The flavour was very good, partly because the dipping sauce was perfect: salt, vinegar, soy. some chilli, a dash of lime. And palm sugar for sweet stickiness and to balance the heat.

Can I drink the water?

Will ice make me sick?

Avoid drinking tap/faucet water. It is rarely contaminated by bacteria or viruses but often contains undesirable levels of naturally occurring heavy metals.

Hotels and restaurants offer fresh and bottled purified water for drinking. In smaller hotels there will be an ultrafiltration unit, often located in the lobby or kitchen. Filling a re-useable bottle saves money, reduces plastic waste, and ensures safe water. In remote areas, it's best to drink from bottles, cans and coconuts. Ice from tourist areas and towns is completely safe because it's made in every town and city from purified water. Avoid ice in remote areas; it may be home-made.

If you are given a warm bottle or can of drink, just look for a fridge, point to it and ask "lahn khom?" (lạnh không?) for 'cold?', or ask "dar khom?" (đá không?) for 'ice?'.

Vegetarian

Vietnamese cuisine is based on lots of delicious vegetables that accompany meat, noodles and rice. Diners choose from several dishes put separately on the table. Restaurants often have a selection of vegetarian options, except some westernized restaurants in the big cities. Because Vietnamese dishes are prepared fresh by the chef, it's usually easy to say "khom dit" for "no meat" or "chay" for "vegetarian" to convert a dish to your needs. It may be worth reminding the staff that fish sauce isn't vegetarian.

Food prices

Everything is surprisingly cheap – some of the best prices in southeast Asia. Bánh mì, phở, cốm rán cost $1-$3 each, drip coffee and local beers are $1 and espressos and imported beers are $2-$4. A top-shelf dinner, such as broken rice with caramelised pork belly, with an added omelette made from two organic, free-range eggs with specialty vegetables costs just $6 (It's called "cơm tấm sườn nướng ốp la" if you'd like to track it down).

The table below shows prices in Vietnam relative to others. An achievable budget for low-cost travellers can be under $10 per day, whereas fine dining costs around $25.

Country	Relative cost of restaurants
Vietnam	$5
Mexico	$8
Thailand	$11
USA	$35
France	$40

Shopping

Markets and shops are easy to find in every town and city. The fun (or difficulty, depending on your outlook) is finding the shop that has what you want. There are few plazas or department stores, but hundreds of separate family-owned shops for kitchenware, manchester, electronics, men's clothes, women's clothes, shoes and so on.

Shopping for clothing, electrical and other goods can be a great part of any holiday. Even for people who don't normally like shopping. The variety of quality goods is amazing, and the prices can seem unbelievable. Travellers on a budget can buy high quality copies of top-line travel goods for less than half the price of the original items selling in Europe or North America. Check the stitching, buttons and zippers are good quality, so that you know it will last. If the quality of goods is low, it's best to go to another shop rather than bargain for a low price. *The people who get the best discounts compliment the goods and the owner.* The people who complain about prices or quality will miss out.

Snacks and basic foods such as rice, noodles and bread are sold in mini marts (Circle K, MTmart, WinMart *etc*). Many mid-sized grocery stores are co-operatives and have a 'Coop' sign outside. They have more choice, especially of fresh food, and better prices than the minimarts.

My recommendations for your shopping list include anything made in Vietnam or imported in bulk from nearby China. They are unbelievably cheap. Expect to pay just $12 for three metres of premium silk fabric, $4 for a 300 mm shifting spanner, and $40 for an 'áo dài' (the silk national dress, pronounced "owe z-eye" in the north and "owe y-eye" in the south). The more you shop, the better you'll get at it. In tourist markets, begin your purchase by offering 10 to 20% less than the price you are willing to pay.  It's important to work with the seller in a friendly way towards a mutually satisfactory price.

What can you leave off the shopping list? Some locally produced high-end goods are shipped straight to high-income countries and are not available locally. Everything imported from Europe or North America will cost almost the same here because the wholesale price is the same, plus they've paid freight. Savings are possible through low retail and marketing costs for small or lightweight products that are cheap to freight. Gold and gems are priced at international standards, but settings cost much less.

Vietnam is becoming a place for low-cost dentistry and cosmetic surgery. I've had simple dental work done well but advise an abundance of caution: a low price will be quickly forgotten if the dentist or doctor does a poor job.

Everyone should leave time in their itinerary for choosing handicrafts, ceramics, jewellery, paintings and prints. For travellers without much time, the 'Made in Vietnam' chain-stores in the cities sell quality items from village-based, ethnic artisans.

Why are the shops and houses so narrow?

As far back as 1300s, the rulers of Vietnam taxed homeowners and businesspeople according to the amount of street front they occupied. Unless you were rich and wanted to show it off, houses and businesses were built as narrow and tall as practical. Until reinforced concrete and lifts became popular around 1900 it was inconvenient and too dangerous to build more than 4 stories high.

Places to shop	*Best for...*
Hà Nội	Clothes, accessories, craft, propaganda posters
Hạ Long Bay	Pearls
Huế	Folk art, craft, silk
Hội An	Tailored clothes, coffee
Đà Lạt	Fruit, flowers, coffee, craft
Hồ Chí Minh city	Fashion, cosmetics, electronics, jewellery
Cần Thơ	Floating market

Visiting a local booking office can be valuable for finding out the local news. Although guidebooks are popular and contain a huge amount of detail, they focus on the tourist routes. If you love the more authentic and ordinary stuff, ask at these places. They'll know about everything from markets to scenery, festivals and shows. These young travel agents in Huế had good knowledge, good English and great prices for tours and hiring motorbikes.

Health care

Pharmacies ("dee-ehm doo-ohk", tiệm thuốc) provide much of the health care in Vietnam that we expect from doctors. Pharmacists and their assistants listen, ask questions, and dispense medications - no cost for the diagnosis and no prescription. The pharmacists and their assistants often speak English in the cities and do a good job of selling appropriate medications and diagnosing mild illnesses. In addition to the latest pharmaceuticals, there are cheaper traditional remedies that may work well (or not).

See a doctor ("bark see", bác sĩ) for severe, persistent and complex illnesses and minor surgeries. They will make a diagnosis and develop a treatment plan. A shortage of doctors causes long wait times in the public hospital system. Private clinics are less overloaded, and the doctors may be better trained. The cost of a doctor in a clinic is $25 to $40.

In both private and public settings, be prepared to get shuffled from the front counter to a nurse, then a doctor, then a waiting area, then pharmacy or for imaging, then another waiting area, then the payment counter. It helps if a friend or guide can assist you through the process. It is far from perfect, but this is a country of nearly 100 million people on low incomes where everyone is doing their best to care for the sick.

Note: There is no emergency health care on the streets of Vietnam. There are few ambulances, and you should never expect to get one after an accident, no matter how bad. Westerners are given high priority at clinics and hospitals, so your main aim should be to get to one. Tour leaders *should* know exactly what to do.

Hà Nội and Hồ Chí Minh city have private hospitals where you will be attended by knowledgeable doctors. Ask for the 'International', 'French' or 'FV' hospital ("beng vee-en", bệnh viện). Costs are quite low: seeing a doctor is $20-$40, a specialist is $50, an x-ray $15 and a CAT scan only cost me $60. It's common to be discharged quickly, and you'll need to find a hotel for recovery. They will be better staffed and more comfortable than the hospital and will be covered by travel insurance until you're feeling better. If possible, arrange support from your travel companions or through your tour company. If you are traveling solo, ensure that the hotel staff understand your needs: medication, food, clothes, phone and being checked regularly. It's important to make sure that they understand that you are relying on them. An assurance of support is not a useful end of the conversation, particularly if it involves just one member of staff.

***

Essential medications

Iodine solution (Betadine) is a very useful disinfectant and antiseptic for minor cuts and scratches.

Lozenges (Strepsils, Difflam) treat a sore throat. Some contain an anaesthetic or a mild antibiotic or both. Dust, smoke and pollen can be thick in both the cities and countryside. Locals swear by ginger tea ("char goong"), which is available everywhere as fresh tea and as sachets.

Loperamide (Gastro-Stop, Imodium) treats traveller's diarrhoea. But too many will block you up, and don't use it for severe or persistent diarrhoea, which require a doctor.

Anti-fungal cream (Clotrimazole, Canesten *etc*) is for athlete's foot, jungle crutch and ringworm. Wet shoes and a warm climate are a recipe for problems, as is re-wearing  unwashed socks and underwear.

Antacids (Alucid, Gaviscon, Mylanta *etc*) treat reflux and indigestion. These can be the difference between happily dining out and a sleepless night of burning pain. Available in tablets or liquid.

Malaria occurs mainly in central Vietnam. The highlands west of Đà Lạt have the highest risk, where it's wise to use clothing and sprays to repel mosquitoes. Occasional outbreaks may happen elsewhere, too. Medications are effective but the cheap ones have the worst side effects, and the others are quite expensive. Talk to a doctor at least 4 weeks before travelling, as you may need to start the medication a week or more before leaving.

Travelling with medical conditions

Consult your doctor before departing. In general:

Asthma is well understood, and medication is available.

Contact lenses in Vietnam are almost all for short-sightedness, so if you wear positive dioptre lenses (+1, +2 etc) bring all that you'll need.

Diabetes requires planning. Medication for Type II is available, but only some insulins for Type 1. Please carry or store extra. Try to avoid leaving your insulin to the care of others. "We froze it for your convenience" is real.

Heart conditions and **high blood pressure** need personal attention. Old-fashioned medications are in pharmacies, but newer and expensive treatments and medications may not be available.

Police and security

Vietnam is a safe country for travel. Visitors and tourists from around the world are treated well and looked after.

Tourists and visitors are sometimes worried by the unfamiliar openness and friendliness of Vietnamese people. I remember feeling unsure when first approached by young people asking me to sit with them and answer their university surveys about my travel for their tourism degrees. They seemed too friendly, but there was absolutely nothing to worry about. They were genuine, honest students wanting conversations that will help to improve their grades and give them a chance to use their English skills. If you have time, it's interesting to stop and engage with them. In HCM city, you will see these students in the parks of District 1 and in Hà Nội they're around Hoàn Kiếm lake.

Some minor swindles and thefts do occur in tourist areas, so take a little care. If any disagreements or trouble happens, just ask a Vietnamese person for help. There's no tolerance for anyone upsetting a tourist, and you'll get lots of friendly, supportive help.

Police will be helpful if you have been robbed or injured, but minor scams and retail rip-offs aren't for them. If they are having a quiet day, you might ask if you may pose with them for a friendly photo. They are always impeccably dressed and groomed. Army officers must not be photographed, nor military bases – even if they're in a beautiful garden at a French colonial-era building.

Unfortunately, everyone hears the stories of police issuing inexplicable fines. One such story is that a foreign motorcyclist is fined for not having their headlight turned on. They pay $10, turn their headlight on, and further up

the road are fined $10 for having their headlight on during the day. It's a fictitious story, maybe. If it happens to you, don't start a long discussion about the law or the facts, as the situation won't improve.

Recently, traffic fines have been changed to an electronic system paid centrally, rather than collected on the spot. At the time of writing, it was still new. Time will tell how it fits into the system of policing overall.

The relationship between traffic police and the rest of us reminds me of cats and mice. Smart mice don't ever annoy a cat, and nothing attracts cats more than two mice squeaking and fighting. When caught in the claws of a cat, the smart mouse plays dead. Lucky for the mice, cats just want to milk them, then let them go. The mice don't like it, but it's better than being eaten. Vietnamese cats grow sleek and fat on a steady supply of milk.

***

Illegal drugs: Việt Nam has severe penalties for possessing, using and selling a wide range of drugs. Life imprisonment and the death penalty are not just possible; they happen quite a lot.

Please be aware of any suspicious activity around you and your bags, especially when crossing borders. I use small, bright red locks on my bags to highlight to any drug smuggler or thief that my gear isn't easy to get into without causing obvious damage.

Transport

Budget airlines

Budget airlines (such as Vietjet and Bamboo) have tickets that sometimes match the bus prices. They are good for longer trips and well worth considering. Hà Nội to Điện Biên Phủ is a 450 kilometre, 10-hour bus trip. At the time of writing, the flight is just $81 return on Bamboo.

A cheap flight from Hồ Chí Minh city to Đà Nẵng is $80 return instead of a 15-hour bus trip (960 km). Hà Nội to Đà Nẵng is a popular $70 (return) flight of 2 hours each way, replacing 14 hours each way by bus (2 x 770 km).

The main disadvantage of flights is the obvious one that you are stuck onboard and zoom over a lot of interesting countryside and towns.

Buses and minivans

Is it safe to travel by bus and minivan?

Yes. It's the safest and most affordable way to travel on tours, do sightseeing, get between cities and go to remote areas. There are many options, from large deluxe coaches running up and down the freeways, to little old vans running across town.

All buses are ridiculously cheap. For example, Hồ Chí Minh city to Cần Thơ* in a deluxe tourist bus costs around $10. That's a coach seat for a 170 km trip. Self-guided trips on buses can be paced to your needs, are easily rescheduled, and encompass the whole country.

Bus transport in Vietnam has distinct categories, depending  on budget, comfort and distances. Deluxe tourist buses are the top-shelf service, minivans take small groups in air-conditioned comfort, intercity buses do long trips at low prices and city buses are for cheap and crowded commuting.

---

*Traveling into the Mekong Delta on a bus from Hồ Chí Minh city to Cần Thơ is a "must do" trip. There's a bunch of experiences and attractions to keep you busy for at least 2 or 3 days: Phong Điền market, the famous Cái Răng floating market, Ông temple, Bằng Lăng stork gardens Tây Đô night market and the history of Bình Thủy house.

Deluxe (Express) tourist buses operate frequently between the major cities. These are non-smoking, have about fifty comfortable seats, air-conditioning and Wi-Fi. There may be a conductor who speaks some English and hands out water bottles and snacks. Luggage goes underneath, out of the rain, but it may get covered in dust. Expect to pay $4-7 per 100 km. For a very reasonable fee they will also carry large items such as a surfboard, bicycle or even a motorbike.

In the cities you will be picked up in a car or minivan first and delivered to the main bus station (usually included in the ticket price). Your deluxe bus will stop for toilets, drinks and snacks every 1½ to 2 hours. Take note of your buses' number plate, as there might be several in the carpark and they're sometimes moved around.

Booking a deluxe bus is easy via your accommodation, a booking office or online (usually a bit cheaper). Be sure to print a paper copy of your ticket. "Open tickets" allow travel across a network, such as 14 days with four stops. These are especially popular for the trip from Hồ Chí Minh city to Hà Nội.

Reputable companies operating across Việt Nam include Mai Linh Express and The Sinh Tourist.

Sleeper buses operate long-distance to several destinations. Usually, there are three rows of narrow, double-stacked bunks. Some people like sleepers because they are relaxing, travel a considerable distance without losing any daytime, and save a night's cost of accommodation. If you are over 178 cm tall (5'11") or over 90 kg (200 lbs) you might not be comfortable in the standard bed, but there may a larger 'group' or "family" bed available near the back of the bus. Sometimes they get filled with luggage, so book early.

Top choices for overnight and slightly longer trips include:

- Hồ Chí Minh city to Đà Lạt. Depart in the morning, to allow a walk or tour in the afternoon. Visit to the markets, waterfalls or "Crazy House" (the cafe across the road has good espresso coffee, too). Stay overnight in the mountain-top city then take a bus to Nha Trang for beaches and beer, then back to HCMC.

- Hà Nội to Mai Châu is 3 hours on a tourist bus (or intercity bus) to a particularly scenic town surrounded by rice paddies and steep mountains. There are quiet homestays, bungalows and hotels among the rice paddies. The town has markets and a mini-mart and a few places to eat. Return to Hà Nội at your leisure.

- Hà Nội to Sapa is a half-day on the bus, delivering you to a magical, mountain-top town. There's trekking, photos, eating, coffee and mingling with ethnic people. There's an international flavour too, with chalet-style hotels, bars, a German bakery, Italian cafes, and Italian pizza and pasta restaurants.

In summary, deluxe tourist buses have the advantages of going faster and further, being more comfortable, being easy to book and pay for, and only rarely running late or breaking down. The main disadvantage is a small one: travelling on the tourist routes. Together these are known as the "banana pancake trail" due to the western influence on the food. Stepping back a street or two from the tourist zones can be rewarding in terms of having a more authentic experience if that is your interest. It's always easy to "spice up" your trip in Việt Nam with some exploring. You won't need to go far.

Minivans make short transfers, such as to and from the bus and train stations and day trips between cities and tourist destinations. For example, Lào Cai train station to Sapa town (north-west of Hà Nội) is a 40-kilometre trip costing $5-$6 (the shuttlebus costs just $2, and a taxi $15).

A seat in a shared minivan from Hà Nội to Sapa is $30 (320 km) or hire the minivan and driver for the day (up to 10 people, ~$200).

Inter-city buses are the workhorses of travel for locals, backpackers and adventurers in Việt Nam. They are mid-sized buses that go almost everywhere at budget prices. They seat 22 to 26 passengers and up to 12 people jammed in the aisle. Some are branded Transinco and other unfamiliar names, but all have superior quality engines and gearboxes (Hyundai, Isuzu *etc*.). Intercity buses require an adventurous spirit and some tolerance of odd and unusual things (one time the driver asked us to get out – which seemed odd until I saw that he was driving around the edge of a cliff because a landslide was blocking most of the road).

Note that some of the drivers are very good, and others are quite scary. It might take a while (or a calming pill) for your nerves to settle when a slightly crazy driver is behind

23

the wheel. In general, if the local people aren't worried, then you can relax.

It is easiest to catch these buses end-to-end (city bus stop to city bus stop) or at a major town because there'll be some help, maybe in English, with ticket prices and destinations. Your luggage is stored under larger buses, while smaller buses have a roof-rack for tying down backpacks, suitcases and sporting equipment. I suggest that you bring or buy a few heavy-duty garbage bags for longer trips, to wrap and keep dust and rain out of your bag or backpack. Watch them get loaded and carry just a day pack onto the bus.

In summary, inter-city buses are complementary to the tourist buses. They are very affordable and provide access to places far off the tourist routes. These buses have Vietnamese passengers, sometimes with a backpacker or two, making for memorable trips.

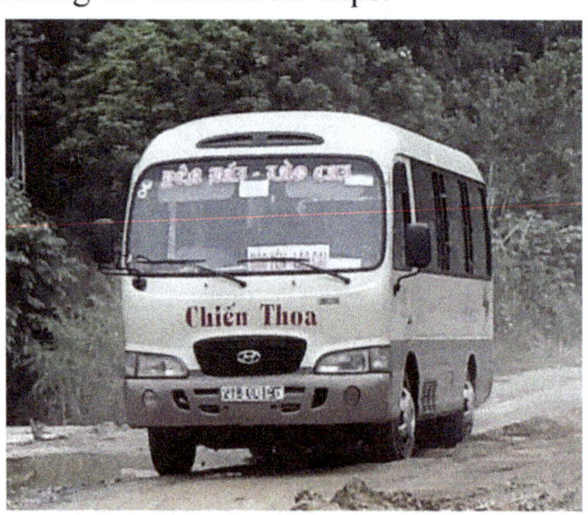

This Hyundai County intercity bus is headed through the far northwest along Highway 12 to and from Lào Cai (written on the windscreen). For $10 you get 300 km on roads through scenic mountains and gorges. Incredible.

Disadvantages include many not running to a timetable. They sit at the bus station until almost full of passengers. They can be noisy, and you might have to stand if you get on the bus mid-trip, after the seats are all taken.

City buses are very economical ($0.20 per km). They are good for working people on their commute and for tourists interested in a communication and navigation challenge. It's a genuine Vietnamese experience, for sure. Not many people take them because moto-taxis, taxis and ride-shares are cheap and easy.

Tips for safety and convenience on buses:

- Ask the price before getting on the bus.
- Do not pay middlemen (who put tourists on a cheap bus after charging a premium price).
- Where possible, board at a bus station.
- Never leave your bags or things unattended.
- Thefts from tourists are often done by tourists.
- Carry snacks and water.
- Want to sleep? An eye mask and earplugs might help.
- Carry hidden cash or a second credit card.

Intercity buses for Hồ Chí Minh city and Hà Nội display the name of the bus stop, so don't expect to see "Hà Nội" or HCM city". Hà Nội has Mỹ Đình, 6 km west of the CBD, Giáp Bát 5 km south, and Yên Nghĩa, 15 km southwest. Hồ Chí Minh city has Miền Đông, located 5 km northeast of the CBD. There are transfer stations too, including one called Cần Thơ that is located 5 km southwest of the CBD.

Walking

As strange as it seems, it takes a day or more to become familiar with walking in Vietnamese cities. When crossing

the road, move at a consistent pace and never step back. Walk with locals and *don't* try to guess what the riders and drivers want to do. It's *their* responsibility to take care of you, and they'll keep you safe.

If you are particularly worried, combine walking steadily with raising your arm to the on-coming traffic, showing the palm of your hand. Like police officers do when they're stopping traffic.

Driving and motorcycling

Cars and **4WDs**: I strongly recommend hiring a driver. Even if a hire company lets you drive, the extra insurance might cost more than hiring a driver. For about $120 a day you get a modern, comfortable 4WD and a good driver/guide. A 4WD is the safest and most reliable way to access rugged and remote areas, such as the south-central highlands (around Đà Lạt), the Red River Valley (upstream from Hà Nội), Đà River Valley, and the spectacular mountains of Hà Giang and Điện Biên provinces. Ask at a booking office for options and prices.

Motorbikes: backpackers and ex-pats ride all around the countryside on a wide variety of machines. It's great fun for anyone with motorcycling skills and a free-wheeling attitude. Almost all riders have awesome trips, but a few have much more enthusiasm than their ability to ride. I recently heard "But she didn't have any accidents in Thailand" after *she* ran head-on into a truck.

For ideas on where to ride, ask at a bike hire shop and check the itineraries that I have included below under Cycling. A comfortable distance for sightseeing motorcyclists is about 150 km per day. It's not much! In Africa, Australia and North America we ride 500-800 km in a day, but in Việt Nam there is so much to stop and see, so

26

many side roads to attractions, so much traffic and so many 
photo opportunities that progress is slow. Sometimes there
will be animals on the road, and a big buffalo can weigh
over 1,000 kg. A good pace for exploring the roads between
Hồ Chí Minh city and Hà Nội is 14 days (including two rest
days with minimal riding).

More good news is that hiring or buying a motorcycle
is quite easy and takes little time. To hire, just pay either a
deposit (about $300) or leave your passport with the
company, in which case be sure to take a copy of the
identification page *and the visa page* and get a receipt for
the original. They might give you a $2 helmet, which is
useless, so get a good helmet (from $40) because your head
and life are worth a lot more than that. You might consider
getting a local license, which involves simple theory (in
English) and an easy practical test with English instructions.

To buy a motorbike, just pay your money and get the
"blue card" that shows you are the registered owner. No
blue card? No deal! Don't accept any excuses or dodgy
deals - it's unregistered because it's stolen or has some other
serious problem. To sell your bike, just exchange cash for
the blue card and the bike. Easy. Note that going from one
city to another decreases the value of the bike, as only
foreigners are permitted to own a bike that has been
registered in another city. It's important to choose a bike
that's popular among foreigners if you'd like a quick sale at
a good price at the end of the trip.

There are four main types of motorbike. *Classics* such as
the Honda Win (110 cc) are bought for their reputation.
Adventurers took Wins into the unknown in the 1980s and
1990s. Those real Japanese-built Wins are rare these days,
but a Thai-built Detech Win will do ok because the roads

are so much better now than 30 years ago. Breakdowns don't matter so much with mobile phones showing maps and making calls. The Chinese copies (the only Wins with electric start) are best avoided, in my opinion. Note that most Wins have crashed and been repaired many times, so they might have bad alignment, bent frames, buckled wheels and other issues of old age and a hard life. Advantages: If you like a bit of adventure and have the skills to assess the condition of the bike before rent or purchase, a classic might be for you. Cheap, fun, easily repaired.

Modern motor scooters such as the Honda Wave (100/110/125cc) offer similar power to a Win, have easier starting, better fuel economy and better brakes. Nice! All have easy-to-use automatic or semi-automatic gears (auto clutch). They are cheap, reliable, and great in town and for short trips. There's nothing better in stop-start city traffic. Photo: Honda Future Neo 125cc ($12/day)

Off-road bikes such as a Honda XR150 or Kawasaki KLX250 are well-suited to longer trips and rough back roads. All have manual gearboxes. They have more power, good suspension, a comfortable seat and front disc brake. Although they're built for rough roads, they're good on the smooth stuff too. These are the best bikes for a 'proper' motorbike tour - unless your budget is very restricted. Bikes over 175cc are more expensive due to a very high import tax, so small capacity bikes are more common.

Photo: Honda XR150 ($25/day)

Small *road bikes*, such as a Suzuki GN125 are good for riders who would ride a scooter, but want a larger fuel tank, wider tyres, disc brakes and don't mind a manual gearbox. They're good on the inter-city roads and highways and ok

29

on dirt roads. Photo: This Taiwanese Sym Husky 175cc was a great bike on the open road. I paid $650 in Hồ Chí Minh city and sold it for $350 in Hà Nội two weeks later. That's equal to $28 per day, plus $6 for mechanical repairs (breaking out two chain links and welding and grinding an exhaust mount).

Cycling

is only limited by how much time and energy you have. The number one choice is a two- or three-day ride in the Mekong Delta ("The Kingdom of the Coconut"). There are no hills, you mostly ride quiet cycling lanes and along picturesque canals, you will have authentic experiences and sample the wonderful fresh produce. Tours are booked online or in Hồ Chí Minh city. Reputable companies offer better trips than budget operators. Two of the best companies that I've toured with are Vietnam Adventure Cycling and Grasshopper Adventures.

Hiring a bike for riding around tourist locations is easy and fun. Sapa and Đà Lạt have hills and cool weather, Đà Nẵng, Nha Trang, Vũng Tàu have beaches, and Ninh Bình has amazing waterways and mountains (to look at).

Booking a cycling tour with foreign companies results in them taking a large booking fee and the tour is then given to a local company. A direct booking or going with a Vietnamese or SE Asian business is cheaper.

30

A good guide is essential. As well as knowing the best routes and sights, they'll look after your bags, food and health and keep you safe.

Photo: Mr Sene of Vietnam Adventure Cycling. We're taking a ferry across part of the Mekong River after

cycling from Bangkok via Angkor Wat in a group of six. We had a driver and 15-seater van for support and back-up. A world-class trip that I would recommend to anyone.

Popular multi-day cycling tours for all levels of experience and fitness include:

- Hồ Chí Minh city to Huế - then train to Ninh Bình or Hà Nội (7-10 days, around 700 km)
- Longer trips in the Mekong Delta (3-5 days, 100 to 400 km).

For experienced cyclists with moderate fitness and resilience, some options are:

- Bangkok to Hồ Chí Minh city via Angkor Wat (900 km). Through modern Thailand then poor Cambodia to Angkor Wat. Explore Phnom Penh, the Cambodian capital, and head east into the incredibly lush and prosperous lands of the Mekong Delta in Việt Nam.

  Unguided, the difficulty is about 6/10 due to patchy Cambodian roads and hot, dry weather in Cambodia's spring and autumn. Best to ride it from West to East

during the cooler months. It's not suitable in summer due to oppressive heat. September to April is ideal.

- Hà Nội to Hồ Chí Minh city (1800 km, best in the dry season). Depart Hà Nội, first for Ninh Bình and the coast. Stay in comfortable cities or interesting smaller towns. The weather and food change along the way. At Nha Trang either take the inland road to Đà Lạt with a 2000+ vertical metres of climbing into the mountains, followed by a great run down into Đà Lạt, or continue to follow easy, quiet coastal roads down to the seaside resort city of Vũng Tàu.

  Difficulty is 7/10 via Đà Lạt or 6/10 via Vũng Tàu. Best to ride North to South in the winter. No problem to do solo for an experienced touring cyclist, but better fun in a group with a guide. Take from 18 days to 28 days.

- Hà Nội to Luang Prabang (800 km). Ride up the Đà River Valley through some of the most scenic countryside in Việt Nam. Go through Hòa Bình, Mộc Châu, Sơn La and across to Điện Biên Phủ near the border with Laos. There are fewer people, towns and facilities in Laos, but some of the roads are amazingly good. Make your way to fascinating Oudomxai (marked Muang Xai on some maps). From Oudomxai either take the road to Pak Beng (one very long day or two short days) and hop on a ferry down the Mekong River to Luang Prabang, or ride direct.

  Touring solo, the difficulty is high (8/10) due to a lack of shops and accommodation in remote areas and negotiating the paperwork, permission and fees at the border crossing to Laos. It's best done in a group with a guide and support, riding east to west.

- Hà Nội to Sapa by bus (300 km) and return the long way (800 km) to Hà Nội. From Sapa go up through Heaven's Gate, down the other side (1500 m descent), then up to the modern city of Lai Châu. Continue along the northern frontier road to Mường Lay and the city of Điện Biên Phủ. Cycling the northern road is usually good but can be tough in bad weather (heat, floods, landslides) or with ill health. A great alternative to cycling the difficult 100 km between Lai Châu and Mường Lay is to catch a bus. Feeling tired? You can bus a little further to Mường Chà, that is just 50 km of scenic hills and one mountain from Điện Biên Phủ. Rest, recover and repair in this delightful, historic city before returning to Hà Nội through scenic Sơn La, Mộc Châu and Mai Châu.

  Difficulty: 6/10 on a tour or very well prepared, or 9/10 going solo and poorly prepared or with bad luck.

A note about provinces, cities, towns and villages

You might notice when searching online maps for a city, the results are for a province with the same name. To get the city, search for 'TP cityname'. An easy way to remember this is: 'TP' is the 'Town that names the Province'.

Smaller cities and towns are 'TT townname' on maps and in searches. They have populations of 2,000 to 200,000 people, so are large enough to have resources including a bus stop or station, some shops and basic accommodation. TX indicates a 'Town that's Xtra small', so check beforehand what's there if you plan to stay.

An epic adventure

Have you already cycled, motorcycled or hiked in Việt Nam and want something tougher, more remote and tremendously rewarding? Maybe you took the 'northern loop' motorbike ride and found it enjoyable, and wonder if there's something more adventurous?

If you've answered 'yes', then there's good news: a little-known adventure that might suit you. It doesn't have a name other than the roads in and out of Mường Tè. Getting to the start is quite a journey on its own. Then the 'heart' of the trip is a side road from Pa Tần through Mường Tè to Mường Lay. If you get to Pa Tần and decide to stay on the highway and avoid the 'serious' bit of the trip, that's a good choice, too. On a motorbike the trip to Mường Tè is a big experience, even if everything goes well. For hikers and cyclists, it's *huge*. In my opinion, it's right up there with climbing Mount Kota Kinabalu (Borneo) or hiking through the Sun Gate to Macchu Picchu (Peru).

How to: From Lào Cai and Sapa, go through Heaven's Pass to the city of Lai Châu. Continue on highway 4D and take note that if trucks are parked near the intersection with the highway to China (QL12), the road is closed somewhere (it used to be common but happens less often now). If all is well, you'll take QL12 straight ahead (i.e., not towards China) to the town of Pa Tần, where you can get basic supplies. Two kilometres past town, the road to Mường Tè is clearly marked on your right (across the bridge). Cyclists and hikers will preferably have a guide and support vehicle from here. It would be a shame to come all of this way, and not complete the trip for lack of support.

Note: it's not far from here to China and Laos. Because of the security situation in this area, taking photos of buildings and people is frowned upon. You might be asked  "No photo" or "No FaceBook" to help avoid problems.

Pa Tần to Mường Tè is only 85 km, but there are two mountain ranges to cross, with almost 3,000 vertical metres of climbing. Despite its remote location, arriving in Mường Tè you'll find shops, restaurants and good accommodation. Returning to Mường Lay is about 120 km down the Đà River Valley. Again, two mountain ranges to cross, but not as high, so it's around 2,500 vertical metres of climbing, and doesn't feel so extremely tough. For most people, 5,500 metres of climbing needs more than 2 days of cycling. Four days plus rest in Mường Tè is good for me. Plan some rest stops, food and water supplies, meals and accommodation.

Be prepared: Sweltering weather can occur anytime except winter, so take lots of water and electrolytes. If you're unlucky, the police (not so obvious) or drug smugglers (obvious) will be around.   But most likely there'll be none of that and you'll just see the best scenery in Việt Nam and enjoy a stunning trip. You'll have noticed lots of villages with traditions from their ancestors. Be aware that in some places, these people speak little or no Vietnamese, using their ethnic languages instead.

Do you have a group of well-prepared adventurers who are keen to do this? Maybe you're thinking "Hell no!" but want to find out more? www.vietnamcoracle.com/the-extreme-northwest-motorbike-guide/ has essential maps, photos, advice and lots of good, accurate information. A donation to them is always welcome.

Note: conditions change fast in the mountains. *Always check before you go*. Good luck and happy adventuring.

Where to go

Most people have limited time for travel, so they take fast-moving tours. The most common goes from Hồ Chí Minh city (HCM city) to Hà Nội via some great tourist stops. In just 10 days you get a lot of sights and experiences. Taken south to north, it goes something like HCM city - Hội An - Huế - Hà Nội - Halong Bay - Hà Nội.

Tours of 14 to 20 days add three or four locations to the list above. They might be Ben Tre, Cần Thơ or Mỹ Tho in the Mekong Delta, Đà Lạt in the mountains, and Mũi Né, Tuy Hòa or Quy Nhơn on the coast. In the north, the additional days are in Ninh Bình or Sapa. These places add depth to the experiences and sights, and I've never heard of anyone regretting taking one of these longer tours. To the contrary – I am often told that one of these places offered a favourite experience.

The tables below are a rough but useful guide to the cities and regions. You'll get detailed information from your tour company that will fill you in on any pre-booked itinerary, or you can search on-line concerning highlights.

****

For people combining short tours, combining a short tour with their own exploration, or building their own itinerary, research is the key to getting a good result. On most trips I wish I'd read more about the places and spent more time working on my itinerary. Have I ever heard anyone say, 'I knew too much before I came'? Never!

My recommended approach to building a tour lasting two or three weeks involves first selecting the region or major city that you can't wait to see. Your heart is set on it, and your energy levels will be high, so it makes sense to go there first. Immerse yourself for a week. When I'm asked  why I recommend a week in just one area, I explain: you can zip from Hà Nội to Hạ Long Bay and back in a day, or from HCM city to the beach at Vũng Tàu. But I don't think many people find this 'tick-a-box' tourism as satisfying as genuine, less rushed experiences. Imagine staying overnight or two nights on Hạ Long Bay or in Vũng Tàu. Following a relaxed evening and restorative sleep, you will wake to the sound of water lapping against the boat, or surf on the beach. Nobody regrets doing those things. So, take plenty of time to know and love each of a few experiences from the 'base' for your trip.

After building a solid itinerary in that city or region, it's time to extend your horizons by considering the connections you want to make to either another focus area or a string of places for stops. From fast-paced, business-oriented HCM city it is easy to connect to Đà Lạt in the mountains, to the tropical Mekong Delta and to central Việt Nam where you'll find the best beaches. The other popular choice is to connect historic, traditional, religious and congested Hà Nội to famous Hạ Long Bay, the mountains of Sapa and scenery of Ninh Bình.

The last stage of building the itinerary is filling in the detail by digging into the online resources and comparing your plans with others.

****

The table below is as simple as a guide can be, but it has been very useful to my busy friends for getting a quick understanding of the major tourist cities and my rating of the "feel good" factor of each. As much as I wanted to separate out the best from the rest, I could not rate any of these places poorly because my experiences have been overwhelmingly good.

If you go to both HCM city and Hà Nội and have a choice of which to visit first, I suggest you go to HCM city. It has quite a few European trimmings, while also having more than sufficient Vietnamese traffic, sizzling street food, noisy music and bustling markets to prepare a first-time traveller for the full-on experience of adorable Hà Nội.

Places	Best for...	Sometimes	Rating
Hà nội	food, tradition,	pollution	●●●●●
HCM city	modern, fun,	heavy rain	●●●●○
Đà lạt	food, modern,		●●●●○
Mekong delta	rivers, food,	heavy rain	●●●●○
Đà Nẵng	beaches, outdoors		●●●●
Huế	history, diversity,		●●●●
Sapa	ethnic, remote	crowds, fog	●●●●

Briefs of the regions

From south to north: It's easy to spend a week in the Mekong delta. There's a lot to do in this tropical paradise of small farms and big rivers. It's the size of Switzerland but has far more people, heat and humidity. It begins just south of Hồ Chí Minh city and extends another 200 km, through twelve provinces, each with a modern provincial capital city. It's known as the 'Kingdom of the Coconut'.

For coastal beachside holidays, look to central Việt Nam. Nha Trang is the place for sunbaking, beaches, nightlife and decadence. Mũi Né is a smaller, funkier place that's a magnet for backpackers on budgets. But there are also some wonderful places that barely rate a mention. Between Mũi Né and Phan Thiết, you'll find some of the best value beach resorts in SE Asia. They have the whitest sand, the cleanest seawater, the least people, and prices about half of Nha Trang. The downside for some people is

a lack of nightlife and limited choices of local bars and 
restaurants. From Nha Trang to the resorts at Phan Thiết-
Mũi Né is about five hours on a nice scenic bus trip going
south along the coast.

Or go up north from Nha Trang to Hội An, which is the
place many people rate the best part of their tour in Việt
Nam, valued for its shopping, architecture, restaurants and
old quarter. On Hội An's doorstep is Đà Nẵng, a liveable
city with endless beachside accommodation, great cafes,
and sandy surf beaches. If you have never tried surfing, the
cheap lessons and great little waves make this the ideal
place to learn.

Huế is just north of here, on the Perfume River. It's the
fortressed, one-time capital of Việt Nam where 250 years
ago an enormous battle raged between the rulers of the north
and the south for control of the country. You can still see
buildings and relics from that era, including a vast fortress.
Some people prefer either Hội An or Huế, but I don't see
one of them as so much better than the other. A few years
ago, I would have chosen Huế, but recent trips to the old
quarter of Hội An have been some of my best experiences
in either. How fortunate then, that it's just a very short trip
from Hội An to Đà Nẵng, and only a slightly longer trip
from Đà Nẵng to Huế. Looking at the three together; there
is a city of culture, a beach city and another city of culture
within just 140 km. They all have excellent food, especially
seafood, and bargains for shoppers.

Because the region north of here, between Huế and
Vinh, suffered very badly from bombing, bulldozing and
spraying during the Second/American Indochina War
(1946-1975), it's often bypassed in tours. This is
unfortunate because the ancient relics and the wartime
histories are thought-provoking. Patches of barren

39

wastelands or ruined buildings may not be attractive to the eye, but they stir the heart and soul.

North from Vinh, Việt Nam expands into the northern region, with Hà Nội the star in the middle. The mountains get steeper, and the valleys get deeper. Ninh Bình is a highlight, with the same limestone pillars as famous Hạ Long Bay. West and northwest of Hà Nội are mountains dotted with small towns, and accommodation catering to every budget. The Đà River valley boasts some of the best scenery in southeast Asia. Popular destinations, from the Hà Nội end going northwest up the valley, include Mai Châu, Mộc Châu, Sơn La and then Mù Cang Chải, which is quite an adventure to reach. Because of stunning terraced hills, winding roads and ethnic minority villages, the area around Hà Giang is becoming very popular for tours out of Hà Nội. It's fun just getting there: 300 km north of Hà Nội and about six hours by bus.

In the far northwest, near the border with Laos is the historic and remote city of Điện Biên Phủ. It's a long way from Hà Nội, an area with considerable poverty and certainly not everyone's 'cup of tea', but I consider it a gem, and absolutely a place that will receive more and more visitors as the years go by. It has an airport, bus station, war museum, a dozen basic hotels and three high-end places. Incredibly, there are a just one or two tour guides with conversational English. The guides cater almost exclusively to Vietnamese groups on package tours. When the surrounding area is so stunning, tourism by English speakers will surely flourish in the future.

Coastal cities and towns offer relaxing resorts with fresh seafood, cheap drinks and swimming pools. Nha Trang is the most popular, while Đà Nẵng is more relaxed, with

40

better beaches and surfable waves. Mũi Né is a funky place and a magnet for backpackers.

A trip to Mai Châu is a popular weekend excursion from Hà Nội, taking 4 hours one-way from a pickup at your hotel. As well as these picturesque scenes, the local White Thai people provide homestays and sell beautiful textiles.

Walking near the river mouth in Phan Thiết was a delight this warm day. It's an interesting city that's not much visited by tourists, who stay at the sandy beaches nearby. However, on rainy or windy days, I think the city is a great place to be. Brush up on your Vietnamese first.

41

	Places	For	Rating
Northwest	Hà Giang, Sapa, Bắc Hà, Ba Bể, Cao Bằng, Điện Biên Phủ	Mountains, rice terraces, ethnic cultures	●●●●●
Mekong delta	Cần Thơ, Bến Tre, Vĩnh Long, Mỹ Tho, Châu Đốc	Rice, fruit, coconuts, jungle, canals	●●●●●
Northeast	Vịnh Hạ Long, Ninh Bình, Cát Bà	Scenery, beaches	●●●●●
Central highlands	Đà Lạt, Buôn Ma Thuột, Pleiku	Mountain air, food, wine, coffee	●●●●○
Red River valley	Mai Châu, Mộc Châu, Sơn La	Farming (rice, fruit, tea, coffee)	●●●●○
South coast	Đà Nẵng, Mũi Né, Vũng Tàu, Phú Quốc	Beaches, resorts, seafood	●●●●○

Confused by place names?

They're quite 'tricky' to pronounce, so check in the table below for the right way (in a Hà Nội accent) to say cities and sights, using familiar English spelling.

Less confused now? Great! Will your friends believe you that these are correct? No guarantees, sorry! Will Vietnamese people understand you better? For sure!

Place	Pronounciation	English spelling
Hà Nội	har noy	Hanoi
Hồ Chí Minh city	hoe chee ming seetee	Ho Chi Minh city
Hạ Long Bay	har long bay	Halong Bay
Đà Lạt	dar lart	Dalat
Nha Trang	nyar charng	Nha Trang
Đà Nẵng	dar narng	Danang
Huế	hh-way	Hue
Hội An	hhoh-ee arn	Hoi An
Sapa	sar-par	Sapa

These 'network' diagrams can be helpful in planning where to make connections on a tour. Travel times can be estimated too, using a rule-of-thumb that 100 km on good roads takes 2 hours in intercity buses and 1 hr 40 in tourist buses. In the mountains, it'll take longer.

The northwest

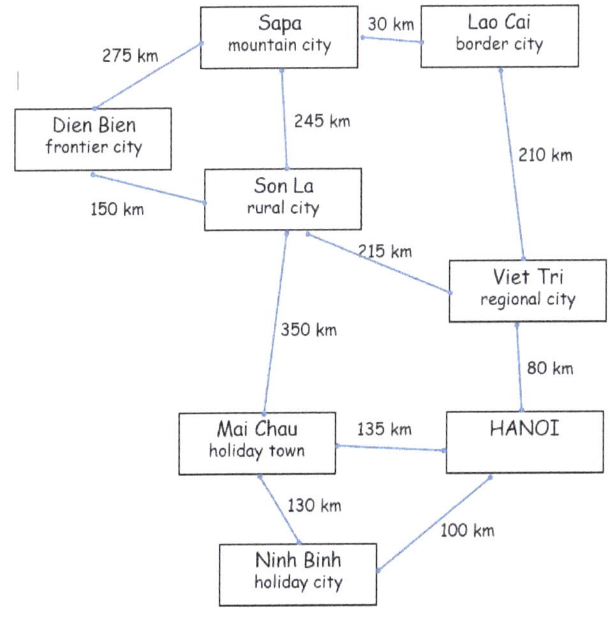

The north

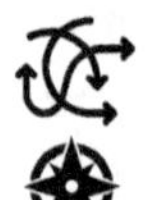

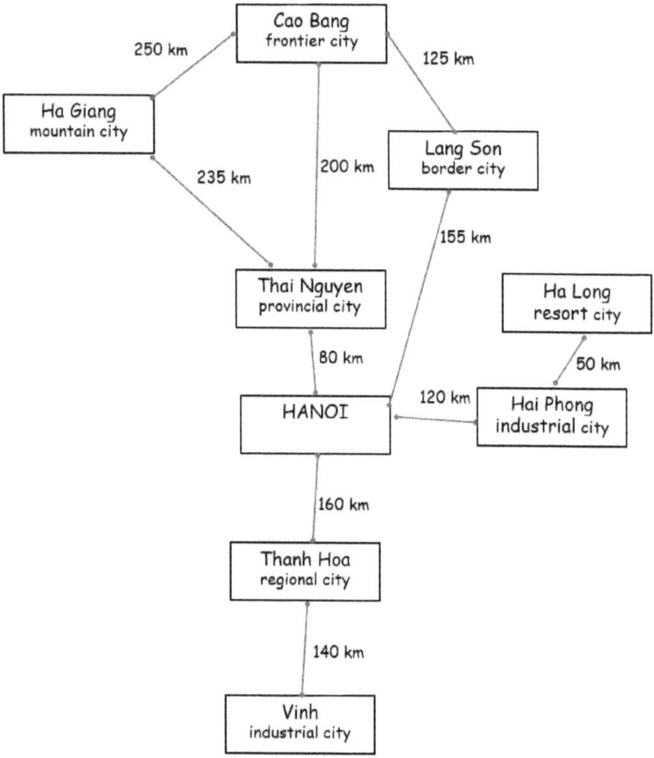
Cao Bang
frontier city
250 km
125 km
Ha Giang
mountain city
200 km
Lang Son
border city
235 km
155 km
Thai Nguyen
provincial city
Ha Long
resort city
80 km
50 km
120 km
HANOI
Hai Phong
industrial city
160 km
Thanh Hoa
regional city
140 km
Vinh
industrial city

The central coast and highlands

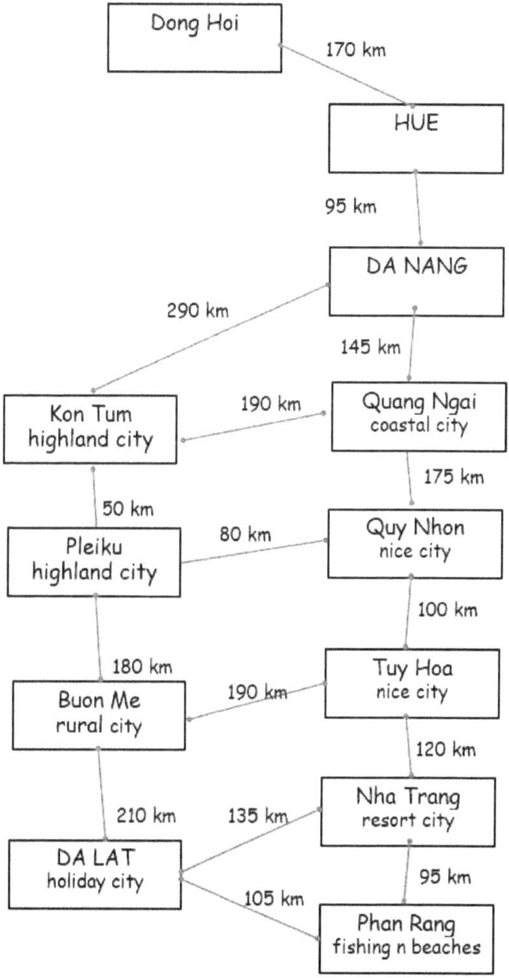

The south

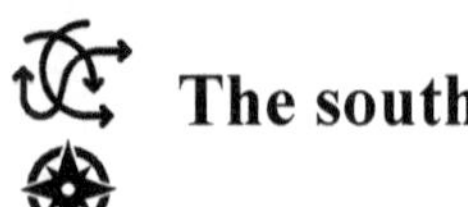

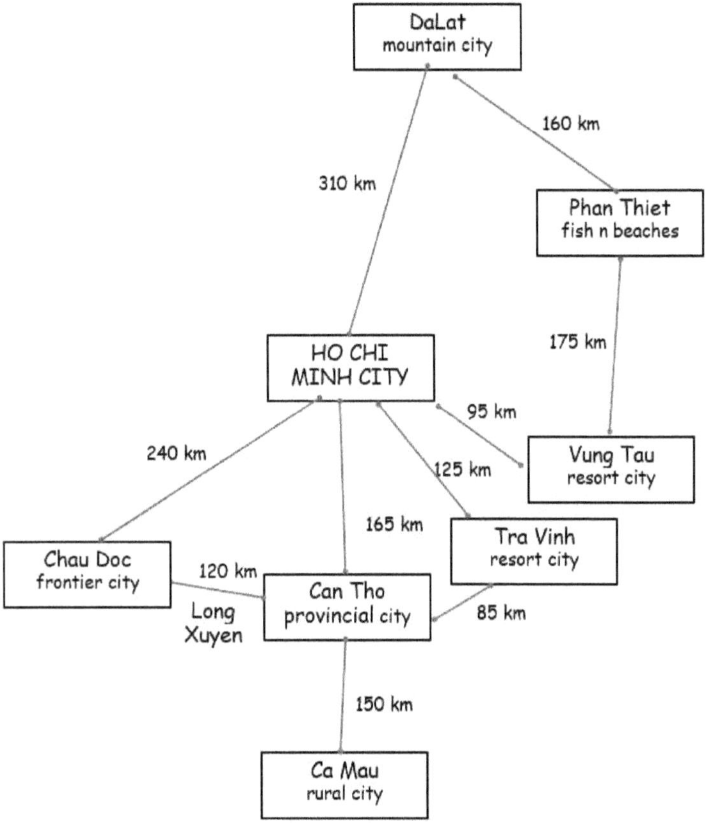
DaLat
mountain city
160 km
310 km
Phan Thiet
fish n beaches
175 km
HO CHI
MINH CITY
95 km
240 km
125 km
Vung Tau
resort city
165 km
Tra Vinh
resort city
Chau Doc
frontier city
120 km
Can Tho
provincial city
Long
Xuyen
85 km
150 km
Ca Mau
rural city

When to go

Travel agents and guidebooks don't say much about the advantages and disadvantages of the main seasons. The table below tries to fill that gap by providing a very quick guide to the calendar, in terms of being outdoors in various places. The weather can be unreliable in the central and northern areas, so you need a bit of luck on your side in addition to good planning.

Place	Best times	
Hồ Chí Minh city	September to May	Wet from Jun to Oct
Hà Nội	August to May	Hot in June
Đà Lạt	All year	
Nha Trang	December to Sept	Wet in Oct, Nov
Đà Nẵng	December to Sept	Wet in Oct, Nov
Hội An	December to May	Hot in June Wet from Sep to Nov
Huế	January to May	Hot in Jun to Aug Wet from Sep to Dec
Hạ Long Bay	All year	Fog in Jan to Mar
Sapa	All year	Fog in Dec to Mar

Note: Hot is 35 C average maximum, Wet is 200 mm average per month

The north has five seasons that overlap at the edges: 1. a cool, foggy winter, 2. a dry and warm spring, 3. a dry and hot pre-summer, 4. a sweltering mid-summer, and 5. a very pleasant autumn. The south is always hot and has just two distinct seasons: the monsoon and the dry season. Despite afternoon downpours on most days, mornings in the monsoon can be cool, clear and very pleasant.

Two to six typhoons affect Việt Nam each year, with one or two causing wind damage and floods. The best

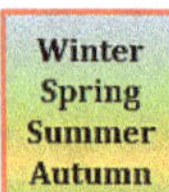

protection is a sturdy old hotel, which will also have sufficient food and clean water for a while.

In greater detail: Việt Nam is hot and tropical, not so different to Manila in the Philippines, Kingston in Jamaica or Cairns in Australia. People from temperate places might find it a shock in summer, but Việt Nam is a winter wonderland. Peak tourist season across the whole country coincides with the northern winter. An average December day in London is a cool 9 C and New York just 7 C, but in Hà Nội it's 22 C. So nice. And Hồ Chí Minh city averages 27 C. Perfect every day.

From Hồ Chí Minh city you can throw on a pair of shorts and a T shirt and head to Vũng Tàu for swimming in the ocean or enjoying an ice-cold beer on the seashore. Although local people say Hà Nội is cold in winter it's warmer than Los Angeles, Casablanca and Athens. Not too bad at all for most visitors

But what about the hot, hot summers? Although Vietnamese people cope well with the midday heat at this time of year, most visitors want deep shade and an ice drink. The hottest days get above 38 C, so take great care of your hydration and electrolytes, use sunscreen and wear a hat. Mornings, on the other hand, are glorious. Many visitors split their days into active mornings, a sleepy siesta, and long languid evenings.

Cooler weather is easily found in the high tablelands and mountains. The best-known temperate cities are Đà Lạt in the south-central tablelands and Sapa in the far northern Tonkinese mountains. They are at 1500 metres above sea level and a wonderful 10 to 15 degrees cooler than the coast. A visit to them shows another side to Việt Nam that most

48

visitors enjoy. The coldest days are below zero. Sapa has occasional snow and reached -6 C on its coldest day.

In the north, the cool weather begins before winter and lasts beyond it. If you would like to avoid the major crowds, consider arriving in September, October or November. This is my favourite time in the northern regions and on the central coast.

Tet, the lunar new year, is a six-day-long celebration and feast for local people. The lead-up has a party atmosphere, but the height of Tet is an incredibly quiet time for visitors because shops, restaurants, tours and almost everything else are shut down. Future dates for Tet are Jan. 22, 2023; Feb. 10, 2024; Jan. 29, 2025; Feb. 17, 2026; Feb. 6, 2027; Jan. 26, 2028; Feb. 13, 2029.

The weeks following Tet are ideal. Everyone feels refreshed and happy, and the whole country is ready for action. The tourist peak is diminishing, so deals can be done on everything. The countryside is also at its green best, with young, green rice crops in the paddies and terraces. My friends ask, "Is it really this green or are you using a filter on your photos?". Yes, it really is very green. Wherever you look. A visual delight.

Travelling in winter shows fields that are mostly empty, and buffaloes and farmers are resting. Rice, corn, soybeans and many of the vegetables only grow in the warm weather. Is it less attractive? Only in the farming lands. The forests, mountains and beaches are usually at their photogenic best in the winter.

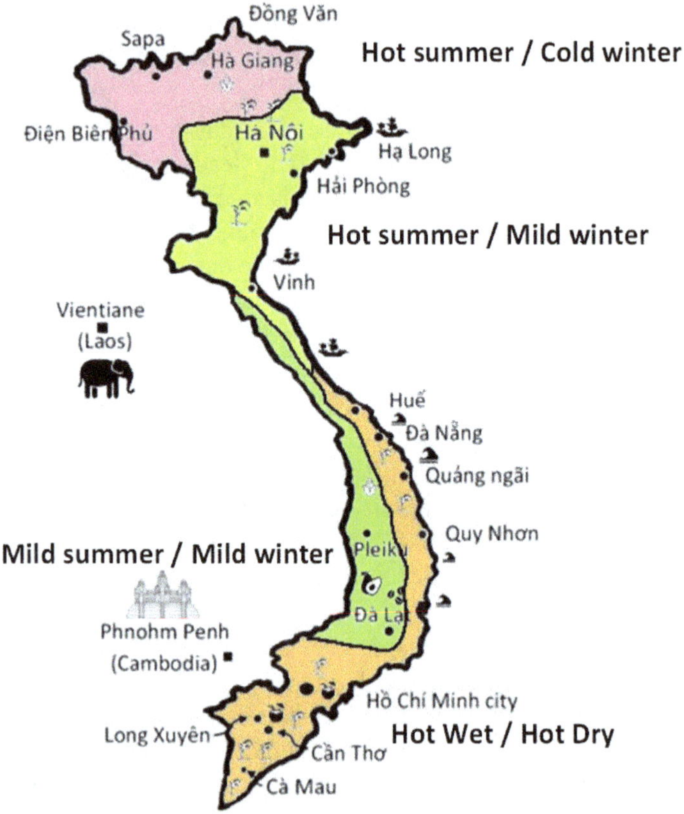

Winter
Spring
Summer
Autumn

Đồng Văn
Sapa
Hà Giang
Điện Biên Phủ
Hà Nội
Hạ Long
Hải Phòng
Vinh
Vientiane
(Laos)
Huế
Đà Nẵng
Quảng ngãi
Quy Nhơn
Pleiku
Đà Lạt
Phnohm Penh
(Cambodia)
Hồ Chí Minh city
Long Xuyên
Cần Thơ
Cà Mau
Hot summer / Cold winter
Hot summer / Mild winter
Mild summer / Mild winter
Hot Wet / Hot Dry

Photos from all over

A picture is worth a thousand words, so there's no better way to tell you about my favourite places than to show you some photos.

But first, an explanation: the internet has thousands of images of popular tourist spots on perfect days. So why am I even thinking of adding my amateur snapshots to those beautiful images? Mainly because the perfect ones show just a fraction of the rich and complex story of Việt Nam. I'll do my best to show the 'other' things – the stuff that local people consider 'everyday' and 'ordinary'. To me, with visitor's eyes, there's surprise and magic at every turn. A kid riding a huge buffalo to school happens every day here, but I always see that and go Wow! Selecting these photos refreshed many happy memories for me, and I hope you enjoy them and their back-stories.

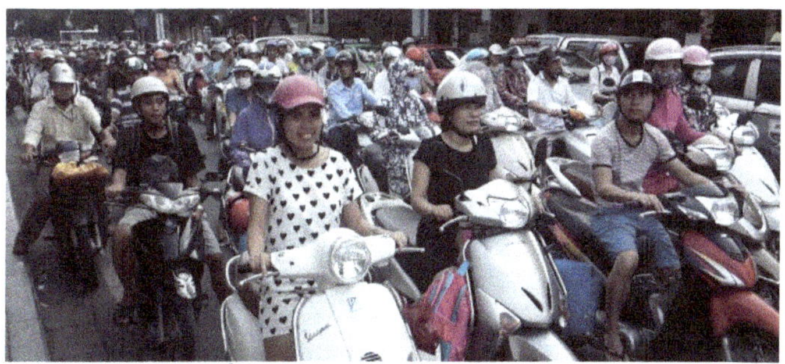

The traffic in Hồ Chí Minh city and Hà Nội has a well-earned reputation for being mad, bonkers and scary. Some people see flow and cooperation, watching with delight and amusement, while others find it chaotic.

From Cát Bà island, this is the view looking towards the outer edge of Hạ Long Bay. Despite it being one of the more popular sea-side escapes, Cát Bà is quiet and relaxed for much of the year. Vietnamese people like to go to the beach in the height of summer (June and July).

In central and northern Việt Nam, flat rice paddies are bordered by steep limestone rocks and mountains. Each valley is well-hidden and distinct from the next, adding surprises and diversity to travel.

Water buffaloes are such big and lovely animals that it always brightens my day to see them. Even with a little calf to protect, this big, muddy mumma was calm and relaxed with me.

There are still a lot of working buffaloes in rural areas.

A "cow machine" is a noisy replacement for the hard-working water buffalo. A four to ten horsepower engine bolts onto a range of devices, such as tractors, trucks, cultivators, pumps and threshing machines.

Ms Mao Thi Chang Chang is a Black H'mong woman living in this valley below Sapa in the far north. We're on a short trek from a village to her mother's home, where we'll have long chats, then vegetables and chicken rice for lunch.

The treks and homestays are unforgettable.

The northern mountains are dotted with farms and an occasional village. Corn is grown wherever steep mountains give way to lesser slopes, while rice and most vegetables are grown on flat land. In some places rice terraces are used to retain water and soil on steep land. Building and maintaining just a few terraces requires a lot of work and dedication. The benefits are high yields, less erosion and a farming system that can last for generations.

The best beaches are in a 600 km stretch between Nha Trang in the south and Huế in the north. The photo shows a beach near Đà Nẵng. Vietnamese people holiday here in the summer, and there's only a few foreigners other times.

The 'inland Halong Bay' of Ninh Bình is just two hours by bus from Hà Nội. A range of accommodation is available, suiting all budgets, in both the city (about 5 km away) and among these waterways through Tam Cốc.

Young people in the cities of Việt Nam love taking photos, shopping for fashion, and eating out. Socializing in small groups is more common than going out as couples.

Going with local people on a shopping expedition is a real treat. There are long conversations (*really long!*) before anything is bought or sold. The photos below are from beautiful Đà Lạt.

Getting to the top of the five-hundred step pagoda near Ninh Bình involves a considerable hike up the stairs. Although it takes a while, there's magnificent views, and a cooling breeze greets you near the summit. It was a grey, foggy day in December when I took the photo, which doesn't do it justice. From March until June, then again from July until November the paddies are a striking patchwork of green.

Tiger Cave at the bottom of the mountain is worth a look. It's not long, but it goes in one side and out the other. Beautiful gardens of bonsai, lotus and water lillies surround bungalow-style accomodation close by.

These Black Thai women are selling cheap and delicious vegetables in a rural market in the north-west (Sơn La). A sizable bunch only costs about $1. Even this meagre amount makes a difference to them and their families. Black Thai kids always look impeccably dressed on their way to school or church and are always interested to see tourists.

In recent years, demand has exploded for power, cable TV and internet connections. Bundles of cables have grown like weeds on the street corners. Is it ridiculous? Yes. Would good planning and regulation have helped?

The secondary road in the photo is one of hundreds perfect for tourists on motorbikes and bicycles. They connect smaller towns. Trucks and buses take the highways.

Millions of kids ride bikes to school, and they're popular for going to the market. Walking and cycling are still favoured in the countryside and might be a reason that people are so fit and healthy. I was introduced to a man in a café near where I took this photo. Though he was 'maybe 100 years old' he chatted away clearly in French, then strolled out the door to walk home. 'How far?' I ask the café owner. 'Four kilometres' he says. 'Four'? 'Kilometres'? Yes, to both.

Drip coffee (cà phê, "gah fay") is delicious and strong. The beans are high in caffeine and more are used, so it's as strong as a triple-shot of espresso. Go easy to start! Condensed milk (sữa, "soo-er") adds a

sugar hit and smoothes the flavour. Fresh milk (UHT treated, sữa tươi, "soo-er teh-ur-ee") may be available too.

Fishing employs and sustains millions of people and generates billions of foreign income (US$) . The net being hauled in here had been set from a small boat in the early morning and contained one or two hundred sardine-sized fish - a few kg. This scene at Sầm Sơn, 170 km south of Hà Nội, is repeated up and down the coast. I joined these workers, who were initially impressed with my size (180 cm, 90 kg). But soon a tiny woman was laughing and saying "big man is not strong enough!" I say "I understand" in Vietnamese and a roar of laughter goes up. Great fun.

A typical rest stop in a mountain pass. This one has a pagoda, fruit stalls and cold drinks waiting in the fridge. For the weary traveler there are little chairs and comfortable hammocks waiting inside and shady trees outside. This one has tropical jungle around it, at Miếu Ba Cô between Hồ Chí Minh city and Đà Lạt.

This day I'm lost. But there's a nice chance to say 'Hi' to the friendly kids. It's 2014 and I was (mis)navigating from a paper map. There's no reason to get lost now, with cheap SIMs and mobile signals reaching almost every corner of the country. Google, Apple, Garmin and OSM maps are all good, and they show an increasing number of ATMs and restaurants and the like, even in rural areas

Rice paddies like these are Vietnam's signature landscapes. Visitors are mesmerized every springtime by the other-worldly emerald green and perfect symmetry. Here in the centre of the north, the fields ripen to gold in June.

If you don't mind a crowd, these markets in rural towns are great fun and totally fascinating. Buyers, sellers, motorbikes, fruit, bread and more are seen crowding into part of this extensive market. On this occasion I've stayed overnight in Bắc Kạn, a small rural city 230 km north of Hà Nội, on my way to Ba Bể lake - the largest natural lake in Việt Nam. It's a beautiful and peaceful place that's popular with Vietnamese tourists. So far, it's not very westernised.

You might see offerings burned on footpaths or streets. They're being sent to the spirit world, for the ancestors to use in the after-life. Among this bunch of offerings are two donkeys and lots of cheaply-printed money.

Fireplaces in the major cities provide convenience for the many people wanting to send offerings. The new moon and the full moon allow closer connection to spirit ancestors, so these are the times when pagodas are busy. Whether you're religious or not, I think you'll find it a joy to see the rituals and family gatherings around any of the thousands of pagodas.

  Be ready in summer with water and electrolytes, a hat or bandana and loose clothing. This June day started out ok for my cycling trip, but soon got very hot. At an isolated shop near Đồng Tâm in Hà Giang province a nice lady beckons me to get under her shady awning. She sits me down, turns on a fan, and gets me a glass of iced water. What an angel. I prefer heat to cold, but it's 39.7 C in the shade and the road is hot enough to cook an egg.

A century ago, in the far north, H'mong kings ruled from a palace in the high mountains. Though humble by European standards, the palace is worth a visit if you're near Hà Giang. There's a sense of bygone grandeur, and ample signs of time, loss and decay. The Kingdom flourished for about 50 years, dissolving when the money ran out.

The 'dragon's backbone' is a line of rugged limestone mountains that run 1800 km from west of Hồ Chí Minh city, up through the centre of the country to the northern border.

This section in central Việt Nam is famous for jungle, mountains and the largest and most beautiful caves on Earth. The nearby town of Phong Nha has accommodation and food, while the pleasant coastal city of Đồng Hới is about 50 km to the south-east.

Phong Nha - Kẻ Bàng National Park is west of the town, extending 25 km to the Laos border. The best attraction in the park is Paradise Cave - it's incredible. There are also underground rivers, and fauna including bears, elephants, tigers and deer. One of the world's rarest mammals lives here: the saola. It's a type of small cow that looks like an antelope and is called the Asian unicorn because it's so hard to find. There's also a legend of a "snake-eating cow" in the mountains. Just one pair of crazy crooked horns is the only evidence that it exists. Hmm.

Đà lạt is the capital of a large province in the southern highlands (Lam Dong). The weather is cool, the air is clean and there are lakes, waterfalls and forests. The food and wine are fabulous. This photo was taken from the Crazy House, built in organic shapes and a rambling style.

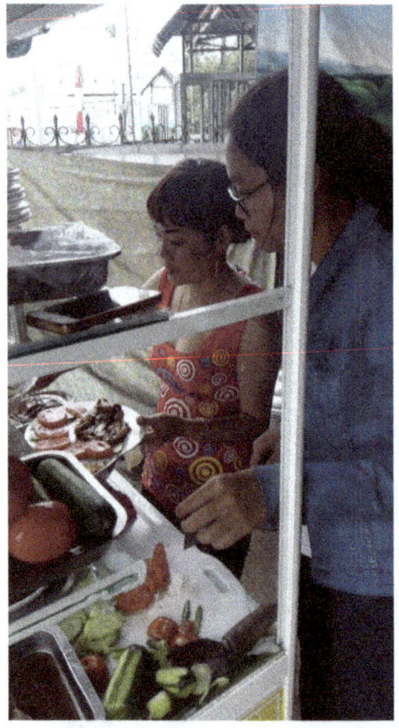

At left, our guide Huyen is making sure our tour group gets bánh mì that are good quality and suit our tastes. A guide opens the country up to travellers, sorting out local issues. Is there a laundromat open? An electrical shop? Where can we find a good lamb hotpot?

Even if you can get around places quite well by yourself or in a group of foreigners, you should consider having some guided days on any trip.

The Chinese writing on this scary sign is illegible to Vietnamese people, but the meaning is clear. The usual fine for crossing is an apology and a few dollars, but the 'death' sign is sure to scare tourists like me away.

Below: Tay Chang is a mountaintop border gate in the north-west. It was a highly skilled woman or man who rode this crazily overloaded 100cc motor scooter up the steep, narrow road with trucks and buses.

Suburban markets (above) and rural markets (below) offer freshness and flavour that aren't available in supermarkets. Tropical fruits lose flavour fast, so if you're from a country where cold storage and long-distance transport are normal, this produce will be a revelation.

Right: Spices, teas, infusions and remedies are piled high in Lan Ong St in Hà Nội. The best smelling street in southeast Asia.

Nha Trang is known for sandy beaches, a mild climate and a party atmosphere. It's also home to the 1,000-year-old Ponagar Cham Towers, a Gothic cathedral, pagodas and sumptuous mud baths.

Dams and lakes are common in the highlands of Việt Nam. Many provide hydro-electric power and water for irrigation. This is Hòa Bình Lake near beautiful Mai Châu, 75 km west of Hà Nội.

Go Lao waterfall is just a few metres from the road to Hòa Bình Lake. Like many natural attractions in Việt Nam, someone has made a parking area ($0.40) and a woman sells cold beer ($1). I ask "Coffee?" and she says "Beer!"

Below: Buffaloes taking it easy on an unusually hot August day (40 C). The people are taking it easy, too, swinging in hammocks under trees and tarps.

Landscapes and Geology 

If we close our eyes and think of Việt Nam, there are a few things most likely to appear in our minds. Towers of limestone rising straight out of tranquil Hạ Long Bay is one of the most common, while others see endless rice paddies ploughed by buffaloes or growing a rice crop so thick it's a green shag-pile carpet. Sometimes these rice paddies are in terraces that climb mountainsides like a giant's staircase. The Mekong delta conjures up dozens of canals and rivers weaving through coconut plantations, fruit orchards, rice paddies and mangroves. Without a hill anywhere.

The nerds among us are always asking "Why is it like this?" and "What explains the things I'm seeing?'. I'm no expert, but nature fascinates me, and I've seen a lot of the country and tracked down a few facts and figures. Let's take a look at the landscapes and how they came to be.

In the far south, the fertile lands of the Mekong delta are the result of thousands of years of floods, with fine sediment transported thousands of kilometres from mountain ranges in India and China. In the far north, the coastal plains east of Hanoi are also the result of erosion far up the Red and Da River valleys in Laos and China. These fertile lands gave rise to the first villages and towns in Việt Nam and many centuries later are still the richest agricultural areas.

The mountainous inland and the coast of central Việt Nam have landscapes where the mountains and valleys are closer: often right next to each other. The soil here is fresh, new, and fertile, created from soft limestone rocks that decompose quite fast when exposed to the tropical weather. That's why the mountains often look so fractured and steep and crooked - like they're falling apart (they are!).

Looking back through time, the minerals that make up today's soil were part of limestone rock a few tens of thousands of years ago. These rocks have been cracking off the sides of mountains, in countryside that looks quite like it does now, for at least two million years. They often fall in tall, narrow pieces after rain cuts deep vertical cracks in the mountains.

The mountains we see now were all part of a limestone slab more than 1,000 metres thick that was lying under the sea until 70 million years ago. That was the time when India pushed north into Asia, raising the Himalayas and lifting the limestone slab to create ancient Việt Nam. The limestone slab under the sea was created from shells and critters in the sea and sediments washing down rivers. This was happening at the same time dinosaurs were around (250 to 100 M years ago). Although limestone is a common rock, there are few places in the world where it is so extensive and exquisitely fractured.

Hạ Long Bay is listed by the World Heritage Organisation because it's such a beautiful and extreme example of this geology. Ninh Bình, often called 'the inland Hạ Long Bay' and Mai Châu are other beautiful landscapes made this way. Together with the flat, fertile Mekong delta, these are the signature landscapes of the country, and visitors are always impressed.

A few places along the central coast have sand dunes and beaches, where the action of the sea and wind has washed out all of the goodness for crops but left the nice clean beach sand of pale silica we like so much.

This is marlstone, a soft rock made of eroded limestone, sand and clay that's been hardened enough to make rock (Photo: near Mai  Châu). It has a high iron content, making it red like rust, with some white streaks of calcium and silica. The limestone that's found almost everywhere in the country was formed under the sea and contains little iron, making grey soils, so this whole valley and mountain range with bright iron-red sandy soil with red rocks really stood out to me as something different. At Mũi Né it might be marlstone that creates the big red sand dunes and red desert soil.

The south-central plateau around Pleiku is known for volcanic rocks, mainly basalt, and deep rich red clay soils that were once forested and now grow coffee, tea and various fruit and vegetables. Other volcanic areas are in the western and northwestern mountains. Outcrops of grey granite boulders and pale rhyolite occur in a few places. In the north, at 3,147 metres, Fanxipan (or Phan Si Pan) is solid granite and the highest mountain in the country. The largest mountain in the Mekong Delta is Nui Sam - a single granite rock that rises to 200 metres.

In some places the limestone of Việt Nam was melted to marble, such as the five Marble Mountains of Đà Nẵng. Other metamorphic rocks, such as slate (melted shale) are more common and are quarried for building paths, walls and other features. Điện Biên Phủ has hillsides with what I think is a highly fractured black shale or gneiss. In any case, after rain it looks amazing, like smashed black glass.

History

I'm sure that anyone reading this chronology will get a sense of how today's Việt Nam was built. But this seven-page summary couldn't present all of the thousands of important events, so those keen on more ancient history should head to the excellent museums in Hồ Chí Minh city and Hà Nội. Visitors are spoilt for modern history that's well presented in the Museum of Hồ Chí Minh, at the Reunification Palace and in the War Remnants museums. The displays are subtitled in English and French.

Pre-history and Chinese rule

~150,000 BCE: Neanderthals and the mysterious Denisovans lived in caves throughout SE Asia, though only a few fossils have been discovered so far. People in southeast Asia and Australia inherited Denisovan DNA, while other Asians and people from many other parts of the world have little or none.

~40,000 BCE: modern humans migrated from the west to settle in China and Việt Nam for the first time. Archeologists are working to recover evidence of both modern and primitive humans, hoping to determine how they lived and why the Neanderthals disappeared.

10,500 BCE: hunter-gatherers lived at Động Người Xưa cave, 120 km south of Hà Nội, using simple tools and communicating in a spoken language. They used stone axes, bone-pointed spears and knives made from oyster shell. Burial sites show they respected their dead.

3000 BCE: tribal and agricultural societies move from either Laos or China to live in the Red River Valley around the site of present-day Hà Nội. Crops were bred for easier

farming and high yields. Animals were tamed and bred to 
provide meat and to replace human labour in the fields.

2000 BCE: the earliest known Vietnamese cave paintings are made, and have many similarities with art in Indonesia, Malaysia and northern Australia.

1000 BCE: a home-grown Vietnamese culture (Đông Sơn) develops in the north, with bronze technology and advanced farming techniques. Around this time the first items are traded between Việt Nam and Europe.

700 BCE: farming, fishing and villages flourish in many locations throughout the Red River valley in the north and the Mekong River delta in the south.

500 BCE: Chinese writings explain how the Việt people, their culture and language are different to China and Laos. Khmer culture develops in what's now Cambodia.

400 BCE: the first Việt people establish in the northern third of modern Vietnam and southern third of modern China (south of the Yangtze River). These are the 'Yu' to the Chinese historians. They war with the Wu to the north.

300 BCE: early Buddhism spreads here from northern India. Many new ideas from earlier religions are added, and some are abandoned. Buddhism then splits into 'schools'.

204 BCE: King Zhao Thuo (Trieu Da) takes 'Nanyue' or 'Việt Nam' from northern China and immediately begins an era of occupation that includes ethnic blending by marrying his soldiers to indigenous Tai-Kadai women.

150 BCE: the Mahayana school of Buddhism spreads through China and Việt Nam.

111 BCE: Han warlords from northern China capture the north and sweep through south-east Asia, changing the cultural landscape of all lowland communities. For the next

thousand years, the Han change the language, law, religion, and characteristics of the people - especially in the north.

111 BCE: Confucianism from China quickly impacts society: personal and social growth, loyalty, order and education are promoted. Partly because they desire order, every future leader of Việt Nam promotes Confucianism.

40 : the three Trung sisters lead an heroic rebellion against Chinese domination. It only lasts three years, but the legend of their bravery is strong in Vietnamese literature and arts.

100 : end of the Đông Sơn culture.

150 : much of Mahayana Buddhism is integrated into Tam Giáo, a religion that also includes Confucian, Taoist and folk beliefs. Tam Giáo coexists with Mahayana Buddhism.

166 : A group of Romans arrive in Việt Nam from Europe.

190 : the Cham empire rises in central Việt Nam. They are Malayo-Polynesian people with strong seafaring traditions and Hindu faith. Their navy and pirate ships are unbeatable.

602 : the Han Chinese rulers ruin economic and cultural development, making themselves the great enemy of the Việt people. Conflicts and uprisings begin.

First independent era

939: under King Ngô the Vietnamese win legendary battles to defeat and expel the Han Chinese to north of the current border, launching the first great era of independence.

1100: Trade between Europe and the orient increases. The quiet Jade Route becomes the hectic Silk Road.

1265: Kublai Khan attacks with 400,000 Mongol warriors and are repelled at the northern and north-western borders.

1288: Marco Polo travels the Silk Road to China and Việt Nam, documenting the cultures and sparking great interest.

78

1300: the Silk Road now links more than 6,000 km of roads from Việt Nam and China to the Middle East and Europe. Traders, diplomats, and priests travel back and forth. 

1474: the Cham rulers lose central Việt Nam to the Trịnh (northern) and Nguyễn (southern) empires.

1627: war breaks out between the Trịnh and Nguyễn. Thousands die in fighting until reaching a truce in 1673.

1775: Huế, the capital of the southern Nguyễn Empire, is captured by the northern Trịnh Empire. A treaty was signed, and the Trịnh army left Huế to southern rebels, who demolished Nguyễn infrastructure and power.

The colonial era

1859: the French navy invade Saigon and the Mekong delta.

1887: the French take control, declaring the new state of Indochina "A colony of protection and exploitation". Slaves work the French rubber plantations, mines and sawmills. Saigon became their principle economic centre.

1893: the French try unsuccessfully to expand Indochina into Thailand, resulting in 20 years of war.

1940: Japan invades and secures the north during the middle phase of their expansion in the Pacific theatre of WWII.

1941: Uncle Hồ Chí Minh forms the Việt Minh resistance to free Việt Nam of foreigners. His first tasks are to assist the USA and European Allies to expel the Japanese.

A call for unity

1945: Hồ Chí Minh writes the Proclamation of Independence of the Democratic Republic of Vietnam. He reads it to a large crowd in Hà Nội, and it's reported around the world.

French War and American War

1946: the British give the south of the country to the French after Japan surrenders. The First or French Indochina War breaks out as the French again invade the north and despite resistance from the Việt Minh led by Hồ Chí Minh the French once again control Indochina.

1954: the French army at Điện Biên Phủ suffer a shock defeat to the Việt Minh, led by General Giap. The French quickly lose control of the north. Anti-communists in the USA say that Vietnam is hungry to invade southeast Asia.

1954: the UN Geneva Conference separates North (with Hồ Chí Minh) and South (with Ngô Đình Diệm). Reprisals begin against landlords in the north and communists in the south. The USA fears the north will align with China into a united Communist power, so condemns the settlement. Vietnam soon aligns with the Soviet Union.

1954: the Second or American Indochina War begins as the USA creates a new government for the south. Citizen paramilitary groups (the Viet Cong) rise up around Saigon to fight against the USA-led southern government.

1963: American support increases for the Diem regime in the South, including thousands of extra military advisors.

1964: a minor naval standoff known as the Gulf of Tonkin incident enrages US President Lyndon B Johnson. He sends in tens of thousands of battle-ready ground troops that increases their number to 184,000. Hồ Chí Minh and General Giap develop plans to be attacked, and to attack.

1967: Soviet support for the north increases as the war intensifies, and the USA responds with several tens of thousands more troops. Khe Sanh is a victory for the USA in central Việt Nam. In the USA the press are given reports of exaggerated and non-existent victories. The actual death toll is kept secret for many months.

1968: the north wins the Battle of Khe Sanh, at a cost of tens of thousands of Vietnamese lives. The USA has 1,500 killed, then the Tet Offensive kills 2,600 more (of 540,000 soldiers). The US generals are pleased and enthusiastic, but the US public are shocked and dismayed by the deaths. 

1970: using pesticides including Agent Orange, USA troops kill much of south and central Vietnam's forests and farms (seven million acres). Four million civilians were doused in pesticides and thousands of people starve. The effects on plants and people will last for up to three hundred years.

1972: public support falters in the USA. At Christmas the USA unexpectedly attacks the north with maximum effort, dropping 20,000 tonnes of bombs on Hà Nội and Hai Phong. The purpose of these brutal attacks is eventually revealed to be part of Nixon and Kissinger's "Peace with Honor" plan that would impress voters, boost morale among evacuating troops, and instill the myth that America chose peace without defeat. However, in the peace negotiations they got no concessions and the north ordered them to leave.

1973: the USA withdraws its troops. Rebuilding begins in the north, quickly spreading south across the old border.

The second independent era

1975: The American Indochina War ends with the exit of Americans and surrender of their government in Saigon.

- Việt Nam is re-unified after 21 years of division
- More than two million civilians were killed
- One and a half million soldiers were killed: 95% Vietnamese, 4% American and 1% others (mainly Laotian)
- Cambodia, a neutral country, was pulverised with 27 million American bombs (more than all of WWII)
- Hundreds of cultural treasures were destroyed.

1975: In chaotic, pulverized Cambodia Pol Pot and the evil Khmer Rouge win the civil war. The Cambodian Genocide begins. No leader has ever inflicted such suffering on their people. Millions are killed, and millions hide in the forests and countryside. The UN and the USA are clueless as to the carnage and support Pol Pot when Vietnamese leaders warn of a humanitarian catastrophe.

1976: Lasting peace in Việt Nam leads to massive road and rail-building projects. The north-south railway is re-opened as the Reunification Line, after 1334 bridges, 27 tunnels, and 158 stations are repaired or replaced.

1978: After 3 years of armed conflict, Việt Nam invades Cambodia and removes Pol Pot and the Khmer Rouge. The genocidal regime and the killing fields are revealed to a shocked world. More than two million people, 29% of the population, were slaughtered by their government.

1979: The UN demands Vietnam's withdrawal from Cambodia and a peaceful settlement is achieved in 1989, ending their second civil war.

1986: The economic opening begins. Doi Moi allows private businesses and marketing. The economic redevelopment of the USSR, East Germany and China follow along similar lines over the next few years.

1995: Việt Nam adds diversity to an expanded ASEAN.

2000: US President Bill Clinton is welcomed on an historic trip to Việt Nam. Relations with the USA are respectful.

2014: Việt Nam enters open conflict with the old enemy — when China increases their occupation of the South China Sea, building artificial islands for military bases.

Religion

Although the Marxist-Communist government doesn't support religions, it happily coexists with them. Devout people are 20 to 40 percent of the population, and almost all follow Mahayana Buddhism, Christianity or Islam. The largest religion, Tam Giáo, the Three Religions Together, places emphasis on personal prayer and actions such as compassion and wisdom. These are so deeply ingrained in people and integrated into society that separating religious and non-religious people is meaningless. Almost all people, including the atheists, have spiritual beliefs. Many young people are 'free thinkers', who ignore religion in the form of books, buildings and leaders, but have personal beliefs.

To better understand, let us go back to the start of religions around the world, then look at Việt Nam in more detail. Thousands of years ago, most cultures believed that plants and animals, the mountains and rivers, and the wind and waves, had a spirit or soul. Some were good and some were evil. There was less distinction between people and nature and spirits. In south-east Asia, scholars separated unthinking nature from living plants, animals and people around 1,000 years ago and went on to decide that heaven is separate from Earth. Although they were very critical of beliefs that spirits affect anyone's lives, few people dared risk their luck, and kept praying for a long and happy life.

This spirituality wasn't just for a religious minority. Then (and now) prayers and belief bring comfort to people in their harsh daily life. An example is that anyone dying young or unexpectedly was believed to be taken by evil spirits. They are jealous creatures and particularly want to take anyone with a kind and generous nature, who was deeply loved by the community.

For many people, the first and fifteenth day of each lunar month are special; a time to visit the pagoda and pray for the departed and take gifts for their afterlife. Fire and smoke carry the gifts to the dead, including banknotes (not real money), cigarettes, a horse or BMW made of cardboard. The most important of these days is Vu Lan, the feast of the wandering souls, when ghosts are released from hell, to walk among us. Prayers assist these souls to be forgiven of past sins so that they can enter heaven.

Photo: A tiger with a slightly angry, human face stands guard at a suburban pagoda. Pagoda have dragons, serpents and phoenix, while temples have even stranger beasts and beast-people.

Spirits made a few occupations very dangerous, requiring special prayers and traditions. For example, fishing from boats far out at sea was prone to bad luck and was an invitation for attack by spirits and the cruel forces of nature. Boats are still painted blue to hide from sea monsters and devil-birds, and huge eyes are painted on the hull to frighten monsters that sneak up from the depths.

An old tradition that faded away is that demons especially wanted to steal the first-born and boys. To fool them, boys were given girls' names, and wore earrings and dresses until puberty. There are still old men who can speak of this fear in their parents and a childhood lived as a girl. I doubt that many people miss these particularly superstitious ideas, so are happy to let them fade away.

As mentioned above, Tam Giáo is particularly common and widespread, but not easy to define because the blend of

beliefs and practices differ from person to person and place
to place. The roots are in quite different beliefs: Buddhism
(the path out of suffering), Confucianism (living an
exemplary life), Taoism (the way of balance) and the folk
beliefs, as described above. Although there was a purge of
Chinese rulers and influences in 939, the Chinese religions
of Taoism and Confucianism continued inside Tam Giáo.
How did they survive? Taoism has sufficient similarity to
Vietnamese folk beliefs that it doesn't seem foreign. And
Confucianism has lots of 'common sense' philosophy that
the rulers after 939 wanted to promote: order, loyalty,
education and moderation. So, Taoism and Confucianism
stayed after other things Chinese were scorned and refuted.

The most common singular religions are Mahayana
Buddhism and Roman Catholicism. Mahayana Buddhism
(The Great Vehicle) emphasises collective wisdom and
consciousness, acknowledges lay people as well as monks,
and teaches that it is possible for all people to reach Nirvana.
Mahayana is the gentle, lenient, inclusive brother of
Theravada Buddhism (The School of the Elders).

The bricks, mortar and wood of religion: you'll see
Catholic cathedrals in almost every large town and city.
The lofty steeples topped by a crucifix can be seen far across
flat coastal countryside. Some are painted bright yellow or
pink, and you'll see architecture borrowed from central
Europe, such as green copper domes (onion domes).

Most pagodas (chùa) are made from wood or brick, and
generally are more modest than cathedrals. People come
and go, make offerings of biscuits, fruit, cigarettes and beer.
These pagodas are places for meeting and relaxing as much
as religion. Out front there'll be smoke trailing from
incense and nearby some statues of long-legged phoenixes
standing on turtles. The gardens are peaceful and green.

Buddhist pagodas associated with monasteries and religious teaching are larger, more ornate buildings of stone, concrete and gold paint. There will be many statues of the Buddha and the protective seven-headed snake-king Muchalinda.

Towers of eight sides and five to eight stories are an older Chinese-style of pagoda that house religious artifacts. A Bodhi tree (*Ficus religiosa*) will be nearby, grown from a piece of the tree in India that shaded the Buddha as he meditated to enlightenment around 530 BC. This style of pagoda developed in India from simple stupas (domes made of brick) used to house the remains of Hindi priests and kings. Many of the Chinese-style pagodas in Việt Nam have survived from the 10th through 16th centuries.

Temples are shrines and stupas. Although people pray at them, their main purpose is to store and celebrate the remains of priests and kings. Beautifully carved stones and bricks on the exterior display Hindi gods, religious symbols, sacred animals and people-animals.

This delightful pagoda (Chùa Tịnh Lâu) is on the West Lake (Hồ Tây) just two killometres from the middle of Hà Nội. Many pagodas are behind high walls, but you are free and welcome to step through the entrance to have a look.

This large, ornate, bright-coloured cathedral is at Nam Dinh, on the coastal plain east of Hà Nội. One of my favourite pagodas, Chùa Keo, is nearby. The Mekong Delta is also a great place for seeing lots of impressive cathedrals.

The Five-pillar Pagoda is a short boat-ride on the Perfume River from historic Huế. It's the ancient style of a multi-level tower with eight sides. There's also a working monastery, splendid garden and historical displays and documents. Regardless of any interest in religion, this is an pleasant and interesting trip.

A very old Vietnamese pagoda at Con Son.

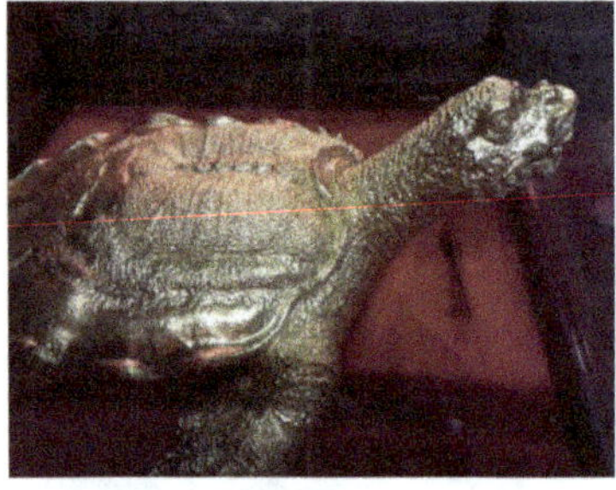

There is a 'Turtle Lake' or 'Lake of the Restored Sword' in the centre of Hà Nội. The legend of the lake is that five hundred years ago a giant turtle provided a magical sword to warrior Lê Lợi, who freed Hà Nội by defeating the Ming Chinese. He became King, and returned the magical sword to the turtle. This golden likeness of the turtle is kept in the pagoda on the lake.

Over the years many people reported seeing a giant turtle. Then…just a few years ago, a turtle was found dead in the lake. An ancient, huge turtle!

Easy Vietnamese

First: it *is* easy. Everyone can do it. If you learn two or three new words each day, usually one of them will 'stick' in your memory. For anyone on a short tour, you'll soon have a wallet of words that you can use in a variety of situations every day.

There are three simple ideas in this section. It's worth looking at them for a minute before getting into some easy Vietnamese. They explain how we'll get started.

One: Learn the sounds. Spoken language is 98% the sounds you make and 2% emotions on your face. As kids we listened and copied over and over until we knew lots of our first language. Five times, ten times, twenty times. With trial and error, we learnt to speak long before we went to school - before any rules of grammar – without a teacher. We had books that we *wanted* to read, not books telling us *how* to read. So - learn like a kid. Say it wrong until you learn to say it right. Be proud of saying new things.

Two: Words are enough. Learning common words gives you a useful and confidence-building experience. You'll use "Hello" and "Thank you", "Yes" and No" everywhere, and the words on the next few pages will add a lot of independence and enjoyment to your trip. Vietnamese people will love you for trying their language.

Three: You can already say it. English has *all* of the sounds of Vietnamese. Some are less common in English, but they're all in there, waiting to be used in the short, strange words of Vietnamese.

❉ If you're doing well, congratulate yourself.

❉ If not… who cares? Nobody! Don't worry about it.

English	What to say	Vietnamese spelling
hello	seen chow	xin chào
thank you	gharm ern	cảm ơn
yes	vung	vâng
no	khom	không
goodbye	dahm bee-et	tạm biệt
so expensive	mawk qwa	mắc quá
I'm sorry	doy seen loy	tôi xin lỗi
excuse me	seen loy	xin lỗi
no thank you	khom gharm ern	không, cảm ơn
my name is...	den doy lah...	tên tôi là...
I'm...	doy lah...	tôi là...
delicious	ngorn lum	ngon lắm
how much?	bough knee-oh?	bao nhiêu?

I don't speak Viet	doi khom noy tee-eng Vee-et
I don't understand	doi khom hee-oh
It was a mistake	chee lah hee-oh lum toy
Where is the toilet?	vay sing oh dow

Drinks and ice-cream

water*	nerrerk	nước
hot	nhom	nóng
cold	larng	lạnh
ice *	dar	đá
Coca Cola	go-gah	coca
beer	beer	bia
wine [red]	zerroh [door]	rượu (đỏ)
fruit juice	nerrerk ep	nước ép
ice-cream	kem	kem

*water and ice are safe in the cities and towns

Common questions and things		Vietnamese
What's your name?	ban dhen zzee	Bạn tên gì?
taxi !	duck see !	taxi !
bus	say boo-eet	xe buýt
train	dao	tàu
bicycle	say darp	xe đạp
motor scooter	say may	xe máy
car	say auto	xe ô tô
hotel	karch sarn	khách sạn
small hotel	nhyar knee	nhà nghỉ
village	larng	làng
directions	who-erng	hướng

Food and drinks		Vietnamese
I want a ...	Doy moo-on mawt...	tôi muốn một...
coffee	gar fay	cà phê
tea	char	trà
black tea	chah lipton	trà lipton
water	nerrerk	nước
orange juice	nerrerk gharm	nước cam
banana	jew-wayee	chuối
orange	gharm	cam
apple	dow	táo
pineapple	zoo-ah	dứa
salt	mur-oo-ee	muối
soup	soop	xúp
soy sauce	nerrerk dow	nước đậu
beef	dit bow	thịt bò
pork	dit lurn / hee-oh	thịt lợn
shrimp	dom	tôm
chicken	dit ghar	thịt gà
egg	chung	trứng
noodles (wheat)	mee	mì
fried noodles	mee shar-ow	mì xào
rice (cooked)	ghom	cơm
fried rice	ghom zzarn	cơm rán
fried rice + chicken	ghom zzarn tit ghar	cơm rán thịt gà
fried spring rolls	nem zzarn	nem rán
spring rolls (meat)	nem dit	nem thịt
fried egg	chung zzarn	trứng rán
vegetable	zzarr-oo	rau

Numbers:

1	mort
2	hi
3	bar
4	bom
5	narm
6	sow
7	bay
8	darm
9	gin
10	moo-ee
100	charm

These numbers can be combined:
400 is bom charm ('four hundreds')
40 is bom moo-ee ('four tens')
12 is moo-ee hi ('ten two')
24 is hi moo-ee bom ('two tens four')

No need to say 'thousand' with money.
40,000 dong is just "bom moo-ee dong".

"1" is hand-written "7" and
"7" is hand-written written "7".
(The French style of writing numbers)

Counting is part of the Vietnamese style of toasting. It's a count to three then shout "cheers!". If the toast includes "charm", they are saying "100 percent" – encouraging everyone to drink it all at once.

one, two, three.. cheers!	mort, hi, bar.. yoh!	một, hai, ba... dzô

Have you or your friends had trouble explaining where you want to go? Most places are pronounced differently to our expectations. The table below gives pronounciations of the larger cities and some tourist attractions. (It's also a useful list for planning and discussing travel, and it can be your 'check list' of places to see, too)

Places (north to south)

Ha Giang	har zzarn	Hà giang
Thai Nguyen	tie new-en	Thái Nguyên
Dien Bien Phu	dien bee-en phooo	Điện Biên Phủ
Hanoi	har noy	Hà Nội
Halong Bay	har long bay	Hạ Long Bay
Hai Phong	hi fong	Hải Phòng
Vinh	ving	Vinh
Hue	hh-way	Huế
Da Nang	dar narng	Đà Nẵng
Hoi An	hoy arn	Hội An
Quang Ngai	kwong nigh	Quang Ngai
Nha Trang	nyar chang	Nha Trang
Dalat	dar lat	Đà Lạt
Bien Hoa	bee-en hwah	Biên Hòa
Ho Chi Minh	hoe chee ming	Hồ Chí Minh
Vung Tau	voong doho	Vũng Tàu
Long Xuyen	long sue-ee-en	Long Xuyên
Can Tho	garn ttur	Cần Thơ

Next level Vietnamese

At this Intermediate level of learning Vietnamese, you're pronouncing common words quite well (like "fur" for phở), but haven't learnt to read Vietnamese, which is a considerable task. But you can go "halfway" to reading.

Have you found that trying to say names from menus, maps and street signs is met with a blank look? It was one of these times that made me decide to improve my reading: About 10 km north of La Gi I ask a roadside seller which of the roads goes to 'Lay Ghee'. They don't understand. Soon I remember 'La' is pronounced 'Larr' and try again. "'Lar Ghee' is where?". She doesn't know and nobody knows. Later, in the town, I discover it's "Larr Zzee". Whoa.

Let's shortcut some of these mistakes in pronounciation for you with a short list of letters that are pronounced very differently to English. These will give you a BIG improvement in being understood.

Basics

't' sounds like the d in d̲irt
'a' sounds like f̲ather ('ar')
'c' sounds like the g in g̲um ('gh')
'g' sounds like the z in z̲ebra ('zz')
in the north, 'r' sounds like the z in z̲ebra ('zz')
in the south, 'r' sounds like the r in r̲oar ('rr')

These will take a long while learn.

Before we go further, let's consider this:

Wait!! Do we aim to become proficient in Vietnamese? No. Being proficient is knowing the Vietnamese for "Zebra" and "Baseline rally" and a thousand other almost useless things (sorry to zookeepers and tennis players). Our aim is to communicate, and we can help ourselves by asking questions such as "What's this?" or saying, "I don't understand" and "I only speak a little Vietnamese".

So, let's check our progress so far and where we might go next. After a long trip or a few short ones, there's a good chance you'll be here in the Next Level. You know and use lots of words and expressions and the table above is helping make sense of menus and signs. If you're ready to go on, then you should learn to read Vietnamese.

At first, I tried quite hard to avoid learning to read. There's a good chance you feel the same. It's discouraging that Vietnamese writing looks messy and unreadable. I changed my mind, and you will too, on discovering that although the writing is messy, the pronounciation is exactly the same as it's written. No silent letters (like 'written' and 'early') and no special combinations (like 'cough').

Learn the letters once, then you can read any word.

Every word and sentence, ask anything, and go anywhere.

English to Vietnamese

The words and phrases in the next pages are written only in English and Vietnamese. The "English that sounds like ok Vietnamese" of the Easy section is left behind now, because learning to read is the easiest way to get good pronounciation quickly. Instead of listening intently and many times, and doing lots of practice for each word, you can get it right in one or two attempts plus a bit of practice. Rest assured, it's not as difficult as some people will say. Usually, they've either never tried or given up when they didn't get immediate success.

You might have already noticed that Vietnamese words are short; just 1 or 2 syllables. It really helps.

> *Vietnamese is one of the easiest languages in the world to learn to read.*

Vowels

There are twelve vowels in Vietnamese. No kidding. Twelve. But... the twelve Vietnamese vowels make just eleven sounds and they're always the same.

Let's contrast that with English, which has just five vowels plus 'y'. And sometimes 'w' acts like a vowel, too (in 'grow' for example, but not in 'growl'). Our five vowels make about twelve different sounds, but not in any consistent pattern. So it takes about ten times longer to learn to read and pronounce English than Vietnamese.

"I'll <u>read</u> a book until I've <u>read</u> it".

"<u>By</u> tomorrow, I'll <u>buy</u> a book and say good-<u>bye</u>.".

Have I reduced your concerns that Vietnamese will be difficult to read? A little? Good. Here are the vowels and their pronounciation using examples you'll already know from English. They're quite familiar, so it's not too hard to learn them. Just spend some time and you'll get them, for sure. They make an enormous difference to the quality of your speech, and you'll need to return to this table less and less as they become natural.

The 12 vowels of Vietnamese

a	father	ă	pat	â	hut
e	pet	ê	pay	i	pee
o	paw	ô	go	ơ	fur
u	put	ư	hoot	y	pee

same

You might try this idea for learning the vowels…

Write two or three vowels on a post-it note and stick it on the fridge or TV

a - father path

ă - cat pat

â - hut nut

Change after a few days.

The 'Ng' sound

If you can say "bang!" you can say the 'ng' sound. Congratulations; that's the most difficult sound in Vietnamese. Bang. Rang, Fang. Some people say it's almost impossible to pronounce. That's nonsense.

People get messed up because the 'ng' is at the start of many Vietnamese words, whereas in English we only have it in the middle or the end. Tip: if you feel the 'ng' as a vibration in your throat, you're doing it just right.

It's a gravelly, growly sound that might seem unfriendly and harsh in other cultures, so we might hear it and think that Vietnamese people are being unfriendly to each other. Not at all. It's normal and happy. It's also in the most common family name in the country: Nguyên.

Tones

Vietnamese is a tonal language because words have meaning that depends on both the letters and the marks above and below the letters. The tones only affect vowels and are marked above or below with five marks: low and falling (à) mid then falling (ả) fall stop rise (ã) high and rising (á) and short fast drop (ạ).

Pronouncing some of the tones is easy for English speakers, such as the rising tone (´) that is similar to the rising tone we use when asking a question in English. Listen to how you say the 'y' in "Really?". That's it. Other tones require practice including the '.' indicating a fast short drop in tone and the ' ˜ ' indicating a fall, stop, rise.

Many words don't have a change in tone, and just some combinations of vowels and tones are more common than the rest. No tone and just one quarter of the combinations make up most common words.

99

A key thing to say now is that *good pronounciation of the letters* will be recognized by a lot of people, *even if the tones are weak or wrong.* Yes, different tones turn '**ma**' (ghost) into '**mạ**' (a rice seedling), but the mistake of saying "I'm afraid of rice seedlings" contains a big clue to the fact that you meant "I'm afraid of ghosts". So, you can often get away with making mistakes, and the bigger the mistake, the easier it might be for people to work out what you mean.

If poor tones meant that words aren't understood, I'd have no chance. So don't worry. A Vietnamese friend told me: "If you don't say anything, you definitely won't be understood". So give it a go, and you're in with a chance

Tone	Mark	Vowels with marks
low and falling	`	à ằ ầ è ề ì ò ồ ờ ù ừ ỳ
mid then falling	'	ả ẳ ẩ ẻ ể ỉ ỏ ổ ở ủ ử ỷ
fall stop rise	~	ã ẵ ẫ ẽ ễ ĩ õ ỗ ỡ ũ ữ ỹ
high and rising	´	á ắ ấ é ế í ó ố ớ ú ứ ý
short fast drop	.	ạ ặ ậ ẹ ệ ị ọ ộ ợ ụ ự ỵ

Learn Vietnamese with Annie

Annie is a Vietnamese woman with a great teaching style and many lessons on YouTube and at her website. Her video 'How to pronounce vowels in Vietnamese' is great. (https://learnvietnamesewithannie.com/). Have a look and if she helps you, consider a donation to say thanks.

Words and phrases

This is a good opportunity to compare the pronounciation you learned by listening and in Easy Vietnamese, to reading them, below. How does it seem? Are they close? Are some easy to pronounce but difficult to read?

The basics again, in Vietnamese	
Thank you	Cảm ơn
Excuse me	Xin lỗi
Hello	Xin chào
Cold water	Nước lạnh
Where's the toilet?	Vệ sinh ở đâu?
See you later!	Hẹn gặp lại!
Oh my goodness!	Ôi trời ơi !

Most people find words like 'cảm' and 'ơn' easy to read. The tricky ones have the unfamiliar nouns together and a tone. At this stage 'nước' looks like a mess, but you've probably said it a lot. Saying it s-l-o-w-l-y while looking at the way it's written is a good exercise. It's n-oo-ur (rising tone) -k. You might not have noticed the rising tone on the 'ur' so much before. This shows why reading can take your pronounciation from good to great.

Thank heavens Vietnamese words are all short and you won't often get a difficult tone together with difficult vowels. Congratulations on making it this far. A huge achievement. I hope you enjoy these word lists and phrases.

People and possession

I	tôi	my	của tôi
You	bạn	your	của các bạn
Him	anh ấy	his	của ông ấy
Her	cô ấy	her	của bà ấy
We	chúng tôi	our	của chúng tôi
They	họ	their	của họ
He	ông ấy	what	cái đó
She	bà ấy	this	cái gì / cái nài
it	nó	that	cái đó

In Việt Nam the words for 'you', 'him', 'her' and 'I' are broken into a lot of categories. At the start, keep it simple and call everyone "bạn" (you). As your Vietnamese improves, you might refer to a man your age as "anh" (brother) and a woman your age as "chị" (sister). On the street you'll hear "chào anh" (hello brother) and "chào chị" (hello sister). There's more; many more, but these are a start. A complete list and details of when and how to use them is in section Bonus 2. More Vietnamese. Speaking to people around you as if they are family members conveys friendliness and warmth. These family-oriented words are part of the extensive social networks, strong social fabric and friendliness of Việt Nam.

Types of things (classifiers)

e.g. buffalo = con trâu, bee = con ong

animals	con	pairs of	đôi
people	người/con	things	cái
plants	cây	vehicles	xe

Surprise! Disbelief!

Are you kidding me?	Bạn đang đùa tôi à?
C'mon!	C'mon!
Oh my goodness!	Ôi trời ơi !

Do you enjoy a joke? Try this: When something goes wrong, say "Ôi trời ơi!" (Oh, my heavens!). If Vietnamese people are around, they'll probably smile or giggle.

After Hello and Thank You, it's the next thing I explain on a tour, and becomes a source of great fun. It's a bit difficult to pronounce, so we get laughs partly because of our terrible pronounciation in addition to the shock and delight of local people hearing it from foreigners.

Coffee and tea

coffee with milk, hot	cà phê sữa, nóng
coffee, fresh milk, hot	cà phê sữa tươi, nóng
coffee with milk, iced	cà phê sữa, đá
black tea	trà lipton

The traditional coffee is quite strong. This is a cà phê sữa nóng. A hot, white coffee, but not very white. Literally: coffee (cà phê), milk (sữa), hot (nóng).

All milk is condensed milk unless you ask for fresh milk.

Buying, selling and paying

How much?
> Bao nhiêu tiền ?

Too expensive!
> **Đắt quá !**

So cheap!
> **Quá rẻ !**

That's too expensive!
> Nó **đắt** quá !

Lower the price, please
> Vui lòng giảm giá

Write the price, please
> Vui lòng ghi giá

I'll give you 10,000
> Tôi sẽ cho bạn mười nghìn

Directions and places

Where is the .... ?	**.... ở đâu ?**
How far?	**Bao xa?**
toilet	**vệ sinh**
ATM	**máy rút tiền**
bank	**ngân hàng**
restaurant	**quán ăn**
fresh market	**chợ**
market	**thị trường**
supermarket	**siêu thị**
hotel	**khách sạn**
guesthouse	**nhà khách**
budget hotel	**nhà nghỉ**

Immigration

passport	hộ chiếu
arrival hall	sảnh đến
work permit	giấy phép
customs	hải quan
TR card	thẻ tạm
PR card	thẻ cư dân

Days, dates, times

today	hôm nay
yesterday	hôm qua
tomorrow	ngày mai
day	ngày
week	tuần
month	tháng
year	năm
last (week)	(tuần) trước
What time is it?	Mấy giờ rồi?
(ten) o'clock	(mười) giờ
half past (ten)	(mười) giờ rưỡi
morning	sáng
afternoon	trưa
evening	chiều
night	tối
next (month)	(tháng) tiếp theo

Weather

it's sunny	trời nắng
lightning	sấm sét
wind	gió
gentle rain	mưa nhỏ / mưa phùn
heavy rain	mưa rào / mưa nặng
it's raining	trời đang mưa
it's not raining	trời không mưa
it's cold (<15C)	trời lạnh
rain / rainy	mưa
storm/ stormy	bão
cold	lạnh
it's cool (18-28C)	trời mát
cloud / cloudy	mây
hot	nóng
flood	lũ lụt
snow / snowing	tuyết

What? Where?

What is this?

    Đây là cái gì?

Where is Hang Bac St?

    Đường nào đến Phố Hàng Bạc?

Students and children

(Cháu = 'young person' : the age of a nephew or niece)

What is your name?

> Tên cháu là gì?

What grade are you in?

> Cháu học lớp mấy?

Do you like sport?

> Cháu có thích thể thao không?

How old are you?

> Cháu bao nhiêu tuổi?

Do you learn English?

> Cháu có học tiếng Anh không?

How do you get to school?

> Cháu đến trường bằng cách nào?

Do you have brothers or sisters?

> Cháu có anh chị em gì không?

Rivers, lakes, ocean

river	dòng sông
lake	hồ
wetland	đầm ngập
bay	vịnh
stream	dòng suối
canal	kênh đào
waterfall	thác nước
small lake	ao
sea	biển
ocean	đại dương

Plants

grass	bãi cỏ
flowers	hoa
tree	cây, cây xanh
vines	cây leo
stem	thân cây
leaves	lá cây
roots	rễ cây
dragon tree	cây thanh long
grape vines	dàn nho

Places

Where is the...?	..... ở đâu?
I want to find a	Tôi muốn tìm một....

eating area	khu ăn uống
ATM	máy rút tiền
streetlamp	đèn đường
building	tòa nhà
shop	cửa hàng
street vendor	bán hàng rong
park	công viên
flag tower	cột cờ
restaurant	nhà hàng
garbage bin	thùng rác
fountain	đài phun nước
bank	ngân hàng

Streets, places and traffic

motorbike	xe ôm / xe máy
car	xe ôtô
bus	xe buýt
bus stop	điểm dừng xe buýt
bus station	ga xe buýt
train station	ga xe lửa
street	đường / phố
bridge	cầu
go left	rẽ trái
go right	rẽ phải
go straight	đi thẳng
repair shop	sửa chữa
traffic	giao thông
traffic jam	tắc đường
intersection	ngã tư
park	công viên
pavement	vỉa hè

Houses and buildings

Where is the...? I want to find a	..... ở đâu? Tôi muốn tìm một....
house	ngôi nhà
airport	sân bay
villa	biệt thự
post office	bưu điện
bakery	bánh ngọt
bank	ngân hàng
pub / bar	bia hơi/ quán rượu
dental surgery	nha khoa
train station	ga xe lửa / ga tàu hỏa
building	tòa nhà / chung cư
pagoda	chùa
factory	nhà máy
small shop	VinMart, Coop, Mart
supermarket	siêu thị
budget hotel	nhà nghỉ
tourist hotel	khách sạn
school (1st, 2nd, 3rd)	trường cấp một, hai, ba
university	đại học

Rice farming

rice field	ruong lúa
rice crop	cây lúa
rice seedlings	mạ
harvesting	gặt lúa
threshing	tuốt lúa
drying rice	phơi thóc
dam	đập nước
canal	trạm bơm nước
pond	ao
ditch / trench	kênh
whole rice	hạt thóc
white rice	hạt gạo
cooked rice	cơm

In the market

Please help me to buy food	Làm ơn giúp tôi mua thức ăn
Where can I buy this?	Tôi có thể mua cái này ở đâu?
When does the shop open?	Khi nào thì quán mở cửa?
I like this	Tôi thích cái này

Food

In larger towns and cities you'll be able to choose between dishes of rice, noodles, pork, beef, tofu, fish, chicken, eggs and many different vegetables. In small restaurants and small towns the choices may be limited. Maybe just rice and noodles with chicken and egg, or with fish, squid and prawns. The 'silver lining' of a restricted menu is that it's local, fresh and appetizing.

Meals

breakfast	ruong lúa
lunch	**bữa trưa**
afternoon tea	**bữa chiều**
dinner	**bữa tối**
a snack	**bữa ăn nhẹ**

In a restaurant

May I see the menu?
> Tôi có thể xem thực đơn không?

What do you recommend?
> Bạn **đề** xuất món gì?

Rice and two fried eggs for me.
> Cơm và hai quả trứng rán cho tôi.

One fried rice and vegetables.
> Một cơm rang với rau

This is delicious.
> Món này ngon / cái này ngon.

Simple, delicious food

fried rice with meat, egg	cơm rang thập cẩm
fried rice with vegies	cơm rang rau củ
fried rice + beef, salted	cơm rang dưa bò
chicken sandwich	bánh mì thịt gà
bread	bánh mì
omelette	ốp lết
spring rolls, fresh	nem (or gỏi) cuốn
spring rolls, fried	nem rán
crispy pancake	bánh xèo
plain rice	cơm tẻ
rice pancake	bánh cuốn
rice noodles and beef	mì gạo và thịt bò
clear soup, beef/chicken	phở bò / gà

Ingredients and options

wheaten noodles	mì ăn liền
pasta	mì ống or nui
cheese	phô mai
onion pickle	hành muối
beef	thịt bò
pork	thit heo (Southern)
	thịt lợn (Northern)
fish	cá
chicken, duck	thịt gà, thịt vịt
egg	trứng
salad	xà lách
fruit	quả gấc
sticky rice sticky	cơm nếp
purple sticky rice	xôi gấc
sticky rice cake	bánh dày
chung cake	bánh chưng
sweet cake	bánh kẹo
peanut candy	kẹo lạc
fruit juice	nước ép
cold water	nước lạnh
with one sugar	với một đường

⭐⭐⭐ My favourite Vietnamese cuisine

Mains

beef mince in betel leaf	bò lá lốt
pork sandwich	bánh mì thịt lợn
lamb hotpot	lẩu cừu
goat hotpot	lẩu dê
meatballs in tomato	xiu mai
stir-fry beef	bò lúc lắc
fried rice & beef	cơm rang dưa bò

Soups and hotpots

clear beef	phở bò
spicy breakfast noodle beef, Huế	bún bò Huế
clear chicken	phở gà
pork meatball noodles	bún chả
shrimp (spicy)	súp tôm
hot and sour fish soup	canh chua cá
thick noodle soup (pork, fish,crab)	bánh canh
snail and tomato (tangy)	bún ốc
crab and tofu (tomato)	bún riêu cua

Light options

spring rolls	nem cuốn / giò cuốn
mini pastie (with egg)	bánh gối
crispy pancake	bánh xèo
(meat, coconut, greens inside)	
morning glory	rau muống
fried rice with egg	cơm rang trứng
omelette	ốp lết

Salads and refreshments

banana flower salad	nộm hoa chuối
lotus root salad	gỏi ngó sen
lhicken salad	gỏi gà
mixed vegie salad	gộm
green papaya salad	gỏi đu đủ
fresh fruit salad	hoa quả dầm
three colour dessert	chè ba màu
smoothie (mango, banana...)	sinh tố (xoài, chuối...)
mango cake	bánh xoài
dried sugared fruit	ô mai

Travel

Accommodation - in detail

Where is a good ...?

    Một (.....) tốt ở đâu?

Can you recommend a (...) please?

    Bạn có thể giới thiệu một (...) được không?

How much for one night?

    Bao nhiêu cho một đêm?

I want a ..	I have a reservation
Tôi muốn một...	Tôi đã đặt chỗ
hotel	longhouse
khách sạn	nhà dài
budget hotel	best hotel
nhà nghỉ	khách sạn tốt nhất
twin room	double room
phòng hai giường	phòng đôi

Communication

How do you say "..." ?

    "..." trong tiếng Việt là gì?

What does this mean?

    Cái này có nghĩa là gì?

What does this word mean?

    Từ này có nghĩa là gì?

Excuse me, please speak slowly.

    Xin lỗi, hãy nói thật chậm

You speak English very well.

    Bạn nói tiếng Anh rất tốt

I'm Jane.

    Tôi là Jane

We are from Australia.

    Chúng tôi **đến** từ Úc.

They're from other countries.

    Họ **đến** từ các quốc gia khác nhau.

I really like Vietnam.

    Tôi rất thích Việt nam.

We are going to Sapa.

    Chúng tôi **đang** đi **đến** Sapa.

We are travelling from Hanoi.

    Chúng tôi **đang** đi từ Hà Nội.

Your baby is so cute.

    Em bé của bạn thật dễ thương.

Oh! Who is this? (to *a friend*)

    Ôi. Ai thế này?

Where is your home-town?

    Bạn quê ở đâu?

Making conversation...

Vietnam people are friendly	Người dân việt nam thân thiện
I like the towns	Tôi thích những ngọn thị trấn
I have visited one time before	Tôi đã đến thăm mốt lần
I am sixty years old	Tôi sáu mươi tuổi
I have one boy and one girl	Tôi có một con trai và một con gái

Light-hearted fun

I don't know how to speak Vietnamese.

Tôi không biết nói tiếng việt.

That's life.

Cuộc sống mà.

It's so boring.

Chán như con gián. ("Boring as a cockroach")

I really don't know.

Biết chết liền. ("Dead before I know")

It's a long way.

Nó là cho đến nay.

I quit.

Bó tay. / Tôi thoát ra.

I'm too tired to care.

Tôi quá mệt mỏi để quan tâm.

You're making it up.

Chém gió. ("Slicing the wind")

You're flirting.

Bạn đang thả thính. ("You're feeding rice to fish")

Are you kidding me?

Bạn đang đùa tôi à?

Vietnamese is hard, I give up.

Tiếng Việt khó quá, bó tay.

Long live the King!

Few people are aware that a kingdom existed in the north 100 years ago. The two Kings served the French for many years, then redeemed themselves and their people with a massive double-cross that helped to free Việt Nam. To better understand the incredible story, I'll go back to the very start, and follow the money trail, because it takes a lot of money for a King to bankroll a kingdom.

In 1545 a Peruvian man discovered a mountain in Bolivia loaded with 40 *billion* ounces of silver (worth $1,500 Billion today). The Spanish got wind of it and took over. To speed up mining, they began transporting the 15 million slaves from Africa who have worked and died in the mine. In 1588 the wealthy Catholic Spanish King (Philip II) used his Armada to attack the Protestant British Queen (Elizabeth). He lost the war and a huge amount of the silver.

Far away, H'mong, Yeo, Black and White Thai people and other ethnic groups were moving into northern Việt Nam to get away from fighting in southern China. For most of the year the mountains are too cold to grow rice or corn, but vegetables and opium poppies do well. Migration increased in the 1800s, bringing more experienced mountain farmers. This would prove to be fortuitous very soon, and it would profoundly affect Vietnamese history.

Back in Britain under Queen Victoria, their wealth in silver was being traded away for tea and spices from China. British silver started to run low, and soon they were in a trade war: wanting Chinese tea but unable to buy or trade for it. Then they hit the jackpot: growing cheap opium in India and shipping it to China. Over the next few decades, the British economically conquered China through the opium trade. Demand for the illicit drug spiralled upwards, out of control, in China during the 1880s. Vast amounts of

silver were traded away to buy opium from India and Việt Nam, where money flooded into the northern communities. Near Hà Giang, a wealthy warlord declared himself King (Vương Chính Đức, 1865-1947) and his son Vương Chí Sình (1886 – 1962) followed, ruling over the opium trade. Opium was a legal, popular painkiller, but the amount being traded was far beyond any legitimate use.

From 1925 the Nationalist government ruled China and worked with drug traffickers buying opium from the King. A great time to be King and a bad time to be Chinese. Mostly broke and struggling to find money to fight the Japanese then Communists, the Nationalists had no shame in pursuing money. Naturally, rebellion grew.

After years of conflict, Mao Zedong's Communists took over Beijing in 1949 and expelled the Nationalists to Taiwan. The King lost his Chinese market, but the French were still buying some from the King and H'mong people and selling it overseas at high prices. This association between the H'mong and the French has long tainted the perception of H'mong people. It unfortunately continues, and next we'll find out why it's just part of the story.

This is a French one ounce silver coin I purchased in the north-west of Vietnam. Melted down, they make beautiful silver jewelry. I've been told that 'H'mong gold' jewellery is made from an alloy of these with Australian $1 copper-nickel coins. This coin with $10 of silver in it sells for just $12.

The King and H'mong and other people now had a stockpile of silver, but they also wanted freedom. Although the French allowed the Kings to rule the opium trade, there was no doubt the French controlled the country. The younger

King inherited the throne and, in an ironic twist, heavily funded Uncle Hồ Chí Minh against the French – using their money! By 1954 when Uncle Ho came to power there wasn't much money left, and the Kingdom fell apart. The Americans arrived and heroin use and addiction ran high among them (around 100,000 in 1970) but all were gone in 1973. The American drug syndicates soon moved away to buy from the Golden Triangle of northern Thailand.

Just as each empire in this story has fallen, the silver itself fell from favour as a precious metal. From Roman times to WWII, silver was worth 1/10th as much as gold. Since then, silver has fallen to only 1/100th of the price of gold, sometimes less. It's just $10 for an ounce.

Today, the H'mong, Dao and other people make good use of their silver for producing jewellery and ornaments. It's resistant to corrosion, workable, and blends with copper, tin and gold. Sellers in Sapa and Hà Giang today make their money from their artistry rather than value in the silver itself.

The discovery of this history involved some luck. I'd been to the silver mine in Potosi, and during a visit to the King's castle, wondered "Where did the King's silver come from? There's not much silver mined here. Could it be from Potosi? How?".

# More travel:

A tour of the Đà River Valley

Over just 13 days this trip explores some of the best mountain scenery, ethnic villages, authentic experiences, culture and history in the north. It can be done faster, especially on a motorbike or in a hired minivan: possibly in just seven days, but in my opinion that's too much time on or in a vehicle. Some cyclists will want to take longer than 13 days. Twenty gives a chance to explore side roads, do some hiking and rest sore muscles.

Tips for motorcyclists: It's cold in the mountains. Take thermals, a scarf, a warm jacket and riding boots. There are repair shops, but take tools, a tube, levers and a pump.

Tips for cyclists: Many of you will need some training beforehand, if not for the 1,000 km, then for the mountain roads. Most days have moderate to steep grades (5 to 9%). A few parts are very steep (more than 12%), and at its highest the air is cold and 20% thinner than usual, so spend at least one night adjusting in Sapa. It's a great town, too.

NB For accommodation at the Pù Luông Ecolodge on Day 10, you must book ahead. It's very popular.

Itinerary

Day 1. Arrive in Hà Nội, the cultural and political capital of Việt Nam. It's a bustling city where traditions are strong, and people are friendly. Assemble or hire your bike, hire a motorbike (Flamingo is good) or plan your bus connections.

Cyclists need to book a tourist bus to Sapa for the next morning, telling them <u>clearly</u> that you are taking a bicycle. 

Mid-priced hotel: May de Ville Old Quarter (43 Phố Gia Ngư, Hàng Bạc, Hoàn Kiếm)

There are dozens of budget and premium hotels.

Day 2. Motorcycle or catch a morning bus with your bicycle up the Red River Valley to Sapa (300 km NW of Hà Nội, 1500 m asl). The town is famous for its mountaintop location and surrounding villages with several ethnic minorities. Sapa and the Tonkinese mountains will be picture perfect if you're lucky.

In the afternoon, take a walking tour up on the mountain above town (allow 2 hours). There's also a bicycle ride down the side of the valley to Thanh Phú. There's a short, sharp hill just before the town, where you'll find water, snacks, beer and coffee. Back is the reverse: a sharp downhill then long solid climb back to Sapa taking up to 3 hours because of the grade, thin air and stopping for photos.

Modest hotel: Dozens of choices. Check some reviews.

High-end hotel: Pao's Leisure Sapa. (out of town)

Day 3. A long and awesome day. Climb 15 km of tough uphill past waterfalls to Heaven's Pass (Trạm Tôn, 500 metres higher than Sapa). There are some coffee and food shops at the top. This is the highest road in the region at 2000 metres asl. On your left is Mt Fanxipan, the easternmost mountain in the ranges that stretch to Pakistan and include Mt Everest and the Himalayas. Next, it's 30 km of nearly continuous downhill, an obvious left turn at the bottom then about 50 km of very enjoyable riding through a rural valley to Thanh Uyên.

Hotel: Ngoc Anh, QL32 (south side of the city)

 **Day 4**. It's an awesome day and a tough day. Follow the road to Mù Cang Chải. There's only one road, which gains about 1,000 metres in elevation before arriving in the town. If the difficult cycling gets too much, there are many scenic stops and a few shops. Short sharp pinches on some corners may involve walking. The motor-scooters have it easy, but the slow pace of a bicycle is good for appreciating the rice terraces, mountains, waterfalls and farms.

Budget hotels: homestays and Nha Nghi in town

Cheap hotel: Mù Cang Chải Ecolodge (10 km East of town, turning at Púng Luông onto the road to Sơn La)

Day 5. Take the wonderful road through a deep and narrow valley going to Sơn La: a compact, modern city and gateway to the Đà River Valley. Today has around 80 km of easy and moderate cycling. Hà Nội is only 270 km away.

Good hotel: Hoa Ban Trắng, Ba Thanh Hai St.

Luxury hotel: Muong Thanh Luxury Sơn La, To Hieu St.

Congratulations! The toughest riding is over. If you're on a motorbike or in buses, spare a thought for the tough and the crazy people who cycled these mountains.

Day 6. Have a rest day in Sơn La. There's an historic prison, easy cycling around town, coffee and good food. An ethnotourism H'mong village (Bản Panh Mong) is about 5 km back up the valley road towards Mù Cang Chải. The mountains that were at your back can be better appreciated now they are in front of you. The H'mong people say these mountains are a sleeping dragon, embracing the river.

Day 7. An interesting day with a lot to see. About 75 km of easy and hard riding on quiet roads. Head southeast out of town. On your right-hand side you can almost see Laos, just 15 km away. Motorcyclists can take the main road to Mộc Châu, but there's a tougher, safer way for cyclists: turn off the highway onto roads 108 and 103. They're not cycled or motorbiked much but are good for keeping you off Hwy 13 with all of its trucks. At about 65 km after leaving the highway, re-join it at Tà Làng. Then it's just a short ride to Mộc Châu, capital of one of the most beautiful provinces in Việt Nam, and famous for its coffee plantations, tea, apricots, rice and fruit. There are many excellent restaurants here.

Fancy hotel: Mường Thanh Holiday Mộc Châu, Đường Hoàng Quốc Việt.

Mid-priced and budget hotels are mainly located in the main street.

Day 8. Mộc Châu to Mai Châu.

How are you doing? Ok? Enjoying the scenery and cultures? Good. Mộc Châu is a favourite of mine, especially in spring and autumn.

Motorcyclists can take even more time today to explore beautiful side roads. For cyclists, my route sounds trickier than it actually is. The route runs parallel to Highway 13, just a few kilometres northeast of it. This keeps you out of the heavy traffic for 27 km before joining it again.

In detail: Please take note of your odometer reading as you leave town. Follow QL43 (not Hwy 13) out of Mộc Châu. Around 6-8 km from town, take "6 alternative" on the right past the gas station. In the next few km ignore the two roads turning off on the right to Vân Hồ (they put you back on lucky Hwy 13 too early). The correct turn is another five km along, at 27 km from Mộc Châu. From memory there's a shop on the corner. Take the right turn then it's only a kilometre down to the highway, turning left onto it. Take the highway with caution until the turn off on your right to

Mai Châu (QL15). It's just a pleasant 5 km ride into town from the turnoff. What a great day!

Big $$$$: Mai Châu Ecolodge, about 2 km out of town.

Medium $: Mai Chau Sunset Resort, 1 km from town.

Budget: a homestay in one of the village stilt houses

Day 9. Stay and enjoy Mai Châu. It's gorgeous from February to October (and nice in winter, too). There's a lot to do here: Touring the flat roads and villages, visiting and shopping in White Thai villages, eating in town.

Day 10. It's very scenic today and only 45 km. But there's a large hill: 15 km with 1000+ m of very tough climbing. Cycle QL15 southeast for an easy 20 km, along the river for 1 km and a bit, then left onto 15C (you can't miss it). Take the steep, winding road for 15 km into Pù Luông Nature Reserve, then enjoy the long, lovely descend for 10 km to a poorly signed turn left into the Ecolodge (Lat 20.45 Long 105.15). It's on a steep hillside with awesome views. There's a swimming pool, bar, restaurant, and other facilities. *Book ahead*.

Fancy hotel: Pù Luông Ecolodge bungalow

Mid-priced: Pù Luông Ecolodge shared longhouse

Day 11. Pù Luông to Tam Cốc (Ninh Bình).

Start fresh and early, as it's a long day for those of us who aren't so young and fit. It's 110 km with a couple of hills and many little rises. Head southeast down from the mountain on QL15C for about 25km and cross the river to meet QL217, turning left and continuing down the valley about 30 km to a dogleg left then right across the river at Phong Sơn. You're heading to Vĩnh Lộc, another 22 km away. The traffic is probably heavier now and you'll see the turn to the left for QL45. After 30 km it ends in a 'T' with busy QL12B, just 20 km from Ninh Binh. It's over behind the big mountains to your east. You're nearly there, but it's complicated now, with little roads going everywhere. If you're fresh and confident, you can follow your nose to the city. Turning right (east) on 12B you can either go ***A***. for 2 km and turn left onto 38C and check a detailed map for the last few km, or ***B***. continue 10 km to QL1, turn left and ride with great care 10 km to Ninh Binh.

Good hotel: Tam Cốc Nature Lodge

Mid-priced: several in town (e.g. Ngoc Anh 1 and 2).

Day 12. A day for cycling, touring and boating in Tam Cốc and Ninh Bình. The staff at your accommodation will have maps and sell tours of the attractions: the row-boat trips, climbing to the five hundred step pagoda, visiting Bích Dộng pagoda and various caves. There's good lakeside cafes and country roads at the northern end of the mountain.

Day 13. Ninh Binh and the countryside here exert a strong attraction, but you'll need to leave sometime.

Motorcyclists will take 3 to 4 hours to get back to Hà Nội. At Phủ Lý you can turn left off QL1 over the river onto nicer QL21B then 4 km later follow it right over the bridge. At the end of QL21B you join Hwy 13 (even busier here).

Cyclists should put themselves and their bike on a tourist bus and enjoy the rest and air-conditioned comfort. IF you must ride, the best option I know is the road along the Red River. You need to go north, avoiding Phủ Lý to your west and Nam Dinh to your east. From the small town of Vĩnh Trụ it's 77 km to Hoàn Kiếm, and easy to navigate. One km east of Vĩnh Trụ, take DT9716 north and after about 20km it becomes 'Đê Sông Hồng' (literally 'Red River Dyke'). Seven km from Hoàn Kiếm you'll go under CT20 and be in the city. Please take great care riding in the city traffic.

I hope you've enjoyed your trip.

More Vietnamese:

Greetings

So far, simple Vietnamese for conversations involving 'I' and 'You' have used Tôi and Bạn. In most conversations and especially in greetings, they are replaced by many words. The easy part is that the Vietnamese words are short; no harder to say than Tôi and Bạn, but there's many of them, varying according to the person's age (or age in relation to you) and gender (sometimes). The examples below demonstrate how to use them. Start with one or two and build up. If you forget: just go back to Tôi and Bạn.

First, some greetings in the English style of "How are you?". The expressions are the same except for the word meaning "you".

Anh có khỏe không? (speaking to a man of similar age to you)

Chị có khỏe không? (speaking to a woman of similar age)

Em có khỏe không? (speaking to a slightly younger person)

Cháu có khỏe không? (speaking to a younger person)

Next is the complete list, demonstrated with greetings in the English style of saying 'hello'. This is a more common greeting in Vietnam than asking 'How are you?'.

If they are the **same age** as you

I is Tôi (slightly formal), tớ, mình (friendly)

you is bạn or cậu

"Hello you" is Chào bạn or Chào cậu

If they are **younger** than you by **less than 10 years**.
I is anh (man) or chị (woman)
you is em, for both
"Hello you" is Chào em
If they are **younger** than you by **more than 10 years**.
I is chú (man) or cô (woman)
you is cháu for both
"Hello you" is Chào bạn or Chào em or Chào cháu

If they are **older** than you by **less than 10 years**.
I is em
you is anh (man) or chị (woman)
"I hello you" is Em chào anh or Em chào chị
"Hello you" is Chào anh or Chào chị
If they are **older** than you by **more than 10 years**, and **younger than your parents**.
I is cháu
you is chú (man) or cô (woman)
"I hello you" is Cháu chào chú or Cháu chào cô
If they are **older** than your parents, and **younger than your grandparents**.
I is cháu
you is bác
If they are the **same age as your grandparents**.
I is cháu
you is ông (man) or bà (woman)
"I hello you" is Cháu chào ông or Cháu chào bà
If they are **around 90 years old**.
I is cháu
you is cụ
"I hello you" is Cháu chào cụ
"I hello you *with respect*" is Cháu chào cụ ạ

Acknowledgements

Tuyen Nguyen guided much of my improvement in speaking Vietnamese. Growing up in a rural town south of Hà Nội, Tuyen excelled at university in Hà Nội and went on to a Master of Education from the University of Victoria, Australia. She teaches English in Hà Nội and has an online book shop for children (Lemon Icecream Bookshop, www.facebook.com/tiemsachkemchanh/).

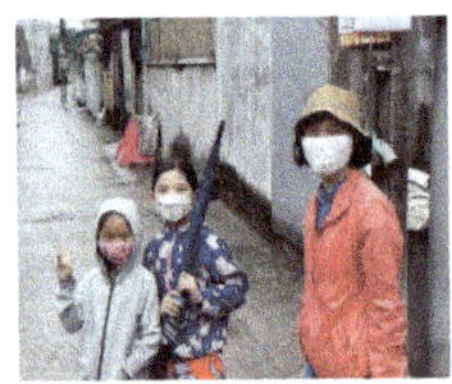

Van Lam edited the Vietnamese language content of this book and made helpful recommendations. I'm grateful for all of her advice.

Linda Nguyen gave me the outline for the Greetings section, and her lessons in Vietnamese pronounciation have helped me considerably.

Thank you all.

About the author

I was born in Brisbane, Australia in 1960. After studying biology and having a career in agricultural and environmental science, I retired from full-time work in 2013. My favourite travels have been in New Zealand, Bolivia, Italy, England and, of course, Việt Nam.

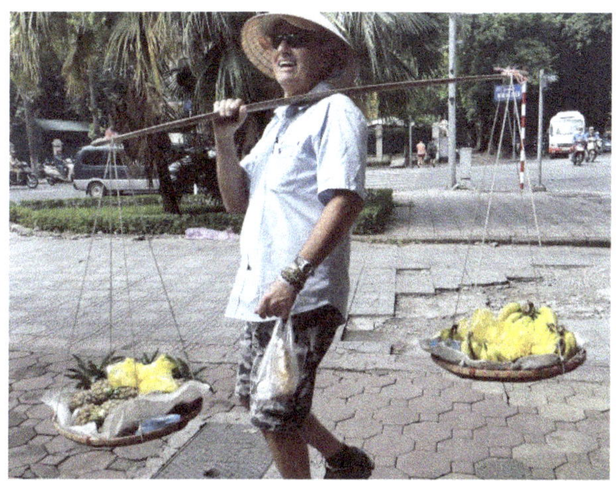

When a street vendor sold me some delicious pieces of pineapple and said I should go around trying to sell fruit for her, I couldn't say no. So, that's me, complete with her 'đòn gánh' (bamboo pole) on my shoulder. She decided I should have her 'non la' (leaf hat) as well.

These bamboo poles bend up and down in time with your walking, so that the load is light when stepping, and heavy when you have both feet on the ground. An ingenious way to carry a heavy load.

Thank you

Should you wish to provide some financial assistance to the children of Việt Nam, I recommend the Save the Children Fund of Vietnam. They achieve consistently high scores from charity ratings agencies, and you can be assured that your money is highly beneficial to poor kids. Every bit helps, even $2 or $5.

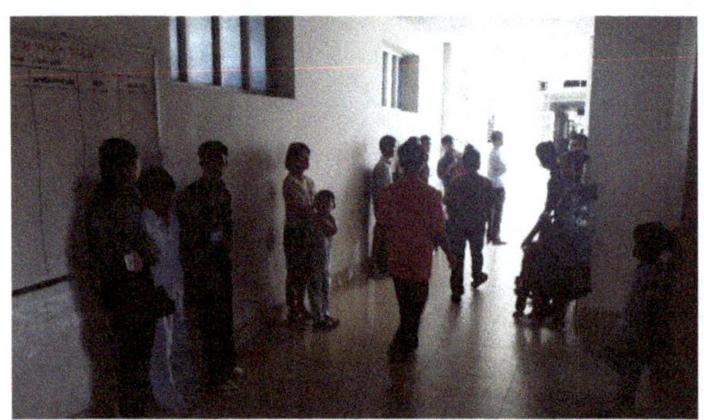

Patients in remote Điện Biên Phủ wait to see a team of volunteer surgeons who travelled overnight on a bus from Hà Nội to provide critical care - free of charge - to poor farming families. Thanks to Quy Kim and Anh Linh for inviting me to the hospital and for your friendship.

Feedback

Please send your comments and suggestions. Email me at **findingvietnam@gmail.com**. I read every one.